**TEACHER'S PET PUBLICATIONS**

LITPLAN TEACHER PACK
for
Dr. Jekyll and Mr. Hyde
based on the book by
Robert Louis Stevenson

Written by
Barbara M. Linde, MA Ed.

© 1997 Teacher's Pet Publications
All Rights Reserved

This **LitPlan** for Robert Louis Stevenson's
Dr. Jekyll and Mr. Hyde
has been brought to you by Teacher's Pet Publications, Inc.

Copyright Teacher's Pet Publications 1997

Only the student materials in this unit plan (such as worksheets, study questions, and tests) may be reproduced multiple times for use in the purchaser's classroom. No other portion of this unit plan may be reproduced in any way without written consent of Teacher's Pet Publications.

For any additional copyright questions,
contact Teacher's Pet Publications.

www.tpet.com

TABLE OF CONTENTS *The Strange Case of Dr. Jekyll and Mr. Hyde*

Introduction	5
Unit Objectives	7
Unit Outline	8
Reading Assignment Sheet	9
Study Questions	13
Quiz/Study Questions (Multiple Choice)	20
Pre-Reading Vocabulary Worksheets	33
Lesson One (Introductory Lesson)	51
Nonfiction Assignment Sheet	55
Oral Reading Evaluation Form	62
Writing Assignment 1	54
Writing Evaluation Form	56
Writing Assignment 2	61
Extra Writing Assignments/Discussion ?s	72
Writing Assignment 3	71
Vocabulary Review Activities	76
Unit Review Activities	77
Unit Tests	81
Unit Resource Materials	113
Vocabulary Resource Materials	131

A FEW NOTES ABOUT THE AUTHOR
Robert Louis Stevenson

STEVENSON, ROBERT LOUIS (1850-1894) Robert Louis Stevenson was born in November, 1850, in Edinburgh, Scotland. He was a sickly child and suffered from tuberculosis throughout his adult life.

The men in Stevenson's family were engineers who designed and built lighthouses and sea lights. While Stevenson was interested in the sea, he had no desire to follow in the traditional family occupation. He was considered a rebel, and disagreed with his family's strict Presbyterian lifestyle. Instead, he completed law school and passed the Scottish bar. Soon after this, he turned to writing as a career, which disappointed his parents. He wrote essays about Edinburgh, which were printed in the Edinburgh University Magazine.

Stevenson traveled frequently both to visit new places and to try and find a comfortable climate for his illness. While in France, he met an American widow named Fanny Osbourne. He went to San Francisco with her and married her in 1880. Both Fanny and her son, Lloyd, encouraged Stevenson to write. His first piece of fiction, a short story called "A Lodging for the Night" was published in 1877.

The inspiration for *The Strange Case of Dr. Jekyll and Mr. Hyde* came to him in a nightmare. Fanny woke him from the dream, and he jotted down as much as he could remember. For the next three days he worked incessantly, and completed the first draft. Fanny suggested that he revise it and present it as an allegory of contemporary Victorian morality.

Stevenson spent his last years living in Samoa with Fanny and Lloyd. He continued to write, even as his health continued to decline. In December of 1894, while working on Weir of Hermiston, he died.

Published Works:
1877 *A Lodging for the Night*, 1878 *An Inland Voyage*, 1879 *Travels with a Donkey in Cevennes*, 1881 *Virginibus Puerisque*, 1882 *Familiar Studies of Men and Books*, 1882 *New Arabian Nights*, 1883 *Silverado Squatters*, 1883 *Treasure Island*, 1885 *A Child's Garden of Verses*, 1885 *The Body Snatcher*, 1885 *Prince Otto*, 1886 *The Strange Case of Dr. Jekyll and Mr. Hyde*, 1886 *Kidnaped*, 1888 *The Master of Ballantrae*, 1892 *The Wrecker* (in collaboration with his stepson, Lloyd Osbourne), 1893 *Island Nights Entertainment*, 1893 *Catriona*, 1894 *Weir of Hermiston* (uncompleted)

INTRODUCTION

This unit has been designed to develop students' reading, writing, thinking, listening and speaking skills through exercises and activities related to The Strange Case of Dr. Jekyll and Mr. Hyde by R. L. Stevenson. It includes seventeen lessons, supported by extra resource materials.

In the introductory lesson, students discuss what they already know about Dr. Jekyll and Mr. Hyde. They also become familiar with 19th century England through a bulletin board activity.

The reading assignments are approximately twenty pages each; some are a little shorter while others are a little longer. They are intentionally short because the vocabulary load in this book is heavy. Students have approximately 15 minutes of pre-reading work to do prior to each reading assignment. This pre-reading work involves reviewing the study questions for the assignment and doing some vocabulary work for 8 to 10 vocabulary words they will encounter in their reading. Vocabulary words have been chosen because they are the ones most likely to appear on standardized tests. Definitions for additional words that will not be tested are also included. You may want to review these with the students prior to reading, or introduce them in context.

The study guide questions are fact-based questions; students can find the answers to these questions right in the text. These questions come in two formats: short answer or multiple choice. The best use of these materials is probably to use the short answer version of the questions as study guides for students (since answers will be more complete), and to use the multiple choice version for occasional quizzes. It might be a good idea to make transparencies of your answer keys for the overhead projector.

The vocabulary work is intended to enrich students' vocabularies as well as to aid in the students' understanding of the book. Prior to each reading assignment, students will complete a two-part worksheet for approximately 8 to 10 vocabulary words in the upcoming reading assignment. Part I focuses on students' use of general knowledge and contextual clues by giving the sentence in which the word appears in the text. Students are then to write down what they think the words mean based on the words' usage. Part II gives students dictionary definitions of the words and has them match the words to the correct definitions based on the words' contextual usage. Students should then have an understanding of the words when they meet them in the text.

After each reading assignment, students will go back and formulate answers for the study guide questions. Discussion of these questions serves as a review of the most important events and ideas presented in the reading assignments.

After students complete extra discussion questions, there is a vocabulary review lesson which pulls together all of the separate vocabulary lists for the reading assignments and gives students a review of all of the words they have studied.

Following the reading of the book, two lessons are devoted to the extra discussion questions/writing assignments. These questions focus on interpretation, critical analysis and personal response, employing a variety of thinking skills and adding to the students' understanding of the novel. These questions are done as a group activity. Using the information they have acquired so far through individual work and class discussions, students get together to further examine the text and to brainstorm ideas relating to the themes of the novel.

The group activity is followed by a reports and discussion session in which the groups share their ideas about the book with the entire class; thus, the entire class gets exposed to many different ideas regarding the themes and events of the book.

There are three writing assignments in this unit, each with the purpose of informing, persuading, or having students express personal opinions. The first assignment is to express a personal opinion: students will keep a journal relating their personal responses to the reading. The second assignment is to inform: students will write a report about a related non-fiction topic. The third assignment is to persuade: students will take a stand for or against Mr. Hyde in the murder trial of Sir Danvers Carew.

The nonfiction reading assignment for this unit will be done in conjunction with Writing Assignment #2. Students are required to read a piece of nonfiction related in some way to *The Strange Case of Dr. Jekyll and Mr. Hyde*. After reading their nonfiction pieces, students will fill out a worksheet on which they answer questions regarding facts, interpretation, criticism, and personal opinions. During one class period, students make oral presentations about the nonfiction pieces they have read. This not only exposes all students to a wealth of information, it also gives students the opportunity to practice public speaking.

The review lesson pulls together all of the aspects of the unit. The teacher is given four or five choices of activities or games to use which all serve the same basic function of reviewing all of the information presented in the unit.

The unit test comes in two formats: all multiple choice-matching-true/false or with a mixture of matching, short answer, and composition. As a convenience, two different tests for each format have been included.

There are additional support materials included with this unit. The unit resource section includes suggestions for an in-class library, crossword and word search puzzles related to the novel, and extra vocabulary worksheets. There is a list of bulletin board ideas which gives the teacher suggestions for bulletin boards to go along with this unit. In addition, there is a list of extra class activities the teacher could choose from to enhance the unit or as a substitution for an exercise the teacher might feel is inappropriate for his/her class. Answer keys are located directly after the reproducible student materials throughout the unit. The student materials may be reproduced for use in the teacher's classroom without infringement of copyrights. No other portion of this unit may be reproduced without the written consent of Teacher's Pet Publications, Inc.

UNIT OBJECTIVES *The Strange Case of Dr. Jekyll and Mr. Hyde*

1. Through reading The Strange Case of Dr. Jekyll and Mr. Hyde students will analyze characters and their situations to better understand the themes of the novel.

2. Students will demonstrate their understanding of the text on four levels: factual, interpretive, critical, and personal.

3. Students will practice reading aloud and silently to improve their skills in each area.

4. Students will enrich their vocabularies and improve their understanding of the novel through the vocabulary lessons prepared for use in conjunction with it.

5. Students will answer questions to demonstrate their knowledge and understanding of the main events and characters in The Strange Case of Dr. Jekyll and Mr. Hyde.

6. Students will practice writing through a variety of writing assignments.

7. The writing assignments in this are geared to several purposes:
    a. To check the students' reading comprehension
    b. To make students think about the ideas presented by the novel
    c. To make students put those ideas into perspective
    d. To encourage critical and logical thinking
    e. To provide the opportunity to practice good grammar and improve students' use of the English language.

8. Students will read aloud, report, and participate in large and small group discussions to improve their public speaking and personal interaction skills.

UNIT OUTLINE *The Strange Case of Dr. Jekyll and Mr. Hyde*

1 Introduction Writing Assignment1	2 MiniLesson Theme PVR Section 1	3 ??s Section 1 Writing Assignment 2	4 PVR Section 2 Oral Reading Evaluations	5 ?? Section 2 MiniLesson Fig. Lang.
6 PVR Section 3 MiniLesson Types of Sent.	7 ?? Section 3 MiniLesson Character	8 PV Section 4 MiniLesson Plot	9 R Section 4 Writing Conferences	10 ?? Section 4 Projects
11 Writing Assignment 3	12 Extra Discussion ?s	13 Vocabulary Review	14 Unit Review	15 Unit Test
16 Nonfiction Presentations	17 Movie			

Key: P = Preview Study Questions   V = Vocabulary Work   R = Read   ??s = Study Questions

READING ASSIGNMENT SHEET *The Strange Case of Dr. Jekyll and Mr. Hyde*

Date Assigned	Assignment	Completion Date
	Story of the Door, Search for Mr. Hyde	
	Dr. Jekyll was Quite at Ease, The Carew Murder Case, Incident of the Letter, Remarkable Incident of Dr. Lanyon	
	Incident at the Window, The Last Night, Dr. Lanyon's Narrative	
	Henry Jekyll's Full Statement of the Case	

STUDY GUIDE QUESTIONS

SHORT ANSWER STUDY QUESTIONS *Dr. Jekyll & Mr. Hyde*

Story of the Door; Search for Mr. Hyde
1. Describe Mr. Utterson and Mr. Enfield
2. While Mr. Utterson and Mr. Enfield were walking, what did they see that reminded Mr. Enfield of an odd story?
3. Summarize Mr. Enfield's story. Include the way Mr. Enfield said he felt about the man.
4. What did Mr. Enfield call the house, and why?
5. What was the name of the man who walked over the child? How did Mr. Enfield describe him?
6. What is the relationship between Dr. Jekyll and Mr. Utterson?
7. Which phrase in Dr. Jekyll's will bothered Mr. Utterson?
8. To whom did Mr. Utterson go to discuss his concerns? What were this person's comments?
9. Describe Mr. Utterson's meeting with Mr. Hyde. Include the way Mr. Utterson felt about Mr. Hyde.
10. What did Mr. Utterson discover when he went to Dr. Jekyll's house?

Dr. Jekyll Was Quite At Ease; The Carew Murder Case; Incident of the Letter; Remarkable Incident of Dr. Lanyon
1. Summarize the discussion between Dr. Jekyll and Mr. Utterson after the dinner party.
2. To whom did Dr. Jekyll compare Mr. Utterson during the conversation?
3. Describe the murder. Tell when it happened in relation to the rest of the story. Give the name of the murderer, the victim, and tell who saw the murder. Describe what the murdered man was carrying. Tell who identified the body.
4. Where did Mr. Utterson and Inspector Newcomen go? Who was there? What did they find?
5. Who gave Mr. Utterson a note? What was the note about? Where was the envelope, and what was unusual about the postmark?
6. What else did Mr. Utterson discover about the note when he talked to Poole?
7. Who was Mr. Guest? What did he discover? What was Mr. Utterson's conclusion?
8. Describe all of the changes in Dr. Jekyll after Mr. Hyde's disappearance. What did he say about seeing Dr. Lanyon again?
9. After a few nights of being refused entrance to see Dr. Jekyll, Mr. Utterson went to visit Dr. Lanyon. Summarize the visit, including what Mr. Utterson thought was wrong. What did Dr. Lanyon say about Dr. Jekyll? What later happened to Dr. Lanyon?
10. Describe the envelope Mr. Utterson receives. Tell who gave it to him, what it says, and what is inside.

Short Answer Study Questions *Jekyll & Hyde* Page 2

Incident at the Window; The Last Night; Dr. Lanyon's Narrative
1. Where did Mr. Utterson and Mr. Enfield go for their Sunday walk? Whom did they see? What happened? How did they react?
2. What did Poole think happened to Dr. Jekyll?
3. Poole said Dr. Jekyll had been asking for something all week. How was he asking for it? What was it? What type did he want?
4. Whom and what did Poole, Bradshaw, and Mr. Utterson find when they broke the door down?
5. Summarize the note Dr. Lanyon received. Tell when he received it, what it said, and who had signed it.
6. Describe the messenger.
7. Retell, in order, the events at Dr. Lanyon's house.
8. How did Dr. Lanyon say he felt after this meeting?

Henry Jekyll's Full Statement of the Case
1. What did Henry Jekyll say his worst fault was? What was difficult about this fault?
2. What did Dr. Jekyll do about his faults and irregularities?
3. In what direction did Henry Jekyll's scientific studies go, and why?
4. Describe, in order, the process Dr. Jekyll went through when he prepared his tincture. Include the results.
5. What was Dr. Jekyll's theory on Hyde's different size?
6. Dr. Jekyll said he had two characters and two appearances. Describe and name each.
7. At one point Dr. Jekyll said he no longer feared the gallows. What horror did bother him?
8. What started happening to Dr. Jekyll the day after he visited Dr. Lanyon?
9. How did Dr. Jekyll describe Mr. Hyde's feelings for him?
10. What conclusion did Dr. Jekyll draw about the original powder?

ANSWER KEY: SHORT ANSWER STUDY QUESTIONS *Dr. Jekyll & Mr. Hyde*

<u>Story of the Door; Search for Mr. Hyde</u>

1. Describe Mr. Utterson and Mr. Enfield
    Mr. Utterson was cold and never smiled. He was tall and lean. He tolerated others, and was more inclined to help than to reprove. Mr. Richard Enfield was more friendly and well known about town.

2. While Mr. Utterson and Mr. Enfield were walking, what did they see that reminded Mr. Enfield of an odd story?
    They were walking on a street and passed a door. The door was blistered and distainted.

3. Summarize Mr. Enfield's story. Include the way Mr. Enfield said he felt about the man.
    Mr. Enfield was on his way home at about 3 AM on a black winter morning. He saw a little man walking eastward, and girl of about 8 or 10 running down a cross street. They ran into each other. The man trampled over the girl and left her screaming on the ground. Mr. Enfield ran after the man and brought him back to the girl. By then the girl's family and the doctor were there. The girl was frightened, but not badly hurt. The man offered money to the girl's family, and they asked for 100 pounds. He used a key to go in through the door. He came back with a check for 90 pounds and 10 pounds in gold coins. The check was signed by a well-known person. Mr. Enfield had taken a loathing to the man at first sight.

4. What did Mr. Enfield call the house, and why?
    He called it Black Mail House. He believed the evil man was blackmailing the man who signed the check.

5. What was the name of the man who walked over the child? How did Mr. Enfield describe him?
    His name was Mr. Hyde. Mr. Enfield said something was wrong with his appearance. He was displeasing and detestable. He gave a feeling of deformity.

6. What is the relationship between Dr. Jekyll and Mr. Utterson?
    Mr. Utterson is Dr. Jekyll's friend and lawyer. He had charge of the doctor's will.

7. Which phrase in Dr. Jekyll's will bothered Mr. Utterson?
    It was the phrase that said if Dr. Jekyll disappeared for any period greater than three months, Mr. Hyde should step into Dr. Jekyll's shoes.

8. To whom did Mr. Utterson go to discuss his concerns? What were this person's comments?
    He went to see Dr. Hastie Lanyon, who was an old friend of Dr. Jekyll's. Dr. Lanyon said he had not seen Dr. Jekyll for about ten years, because Dr. Jekyll had some strange and unscientific ideas with which Dr. Lanyon disagreed. Dr. Lanyon had never heard of Mr. Hyde.

9. Describe Mr. Utterson's meeting with Mr. Hyde. Include the way Mr. Utterson felt about Mr. Hyde.
   Mr. Utterson spent a lot of time near the door until one night he encountered Mr. Hyde. He told Mr. Hyde he was a friend of Dr. Jekyll's, and Mr. Hyde said Dr. Jekyll was not at home. Mr. Utterson asked Mr. Hyde to see his face, and Mr. Hyde complied. Mr. Utterson felt disgust, fear, and loathing for Mr. Hyde.

10. What did Mr. Utterson discover when he went to Dr. Jekyll's house?
    Poole, the servant, said Mr. Hyde had a key and all of the servants had orders to obey him. He also said Mr. Hyde never dined at the house. He came and went by the laboratory.

Dr. Jekyll Was Quite At Ease; The Carew Murder Case; Incident of the Letter; Remarkable Incident of Dr. Lanyon

1. Summarize the discussion between Dr. Jekyll and Mr. Utterson after the dinner party.
   Mr. Utterson told Dr. Jekyll he was concerned about the provisions of the will. He disapproved because of some new information he had about Mr. Hyde. Dr. Jekyll told Mr. Utterson things were not that bad, and he could be rid of Mr. Hyde if he wanted to. He asked Utterson to help Hyde if and when Dr. Jekyll was no longer around. Mr. Utterson reluctantly agreed.

2. To whom did Dr. Jekyll compare Mr. Utterson during the conversation?
   Dr. Jekyll compared Mr. Utterson's concern about the will to Dr. Lanyon's opinion of Dr. Jekyll's scientific theories. Dr. Lanyon had called them heresies.

3. Describe the murder. Tell when it happened in relation to the rest of the story. Give the name of the murderer, the victim, and tell who saw the murder. Describe what the murdered man was carrying. Tell who identified the body.
   The murder took place about a year after the previous chapter. Sir Danvers Carew, a Member of Parliament, was murdered near midnight. A maid was looking out her window and saw the entire murder. She recognized Mr. Hyde, who hit the victim with a cane and then trampled him. Sir Carew was carrying a purse, a gold watch, and a sealed envelope addressed to Mr. Utterson. Mr. Utterson identified the body.

4. Where did Mr. Utterson and Inspector Newcomen go? Who was there? What did they find?
   They went to Mr. Hyde's house. The housekeeper seemed glad to find out Mr. Hyde was in trouble. She said he had come home late and gone away again. The rooms looked like they had been ransacked. They found the other half of the cane that was used in the murder, and a partially burned check book.

5. Who gave Mr. Utterson a note? What was the note about? Where was the envelope, and what was unusual about the postmark?

   Dr. Jekyll gave Mr. Utterson a note from Mr. Hyde. The note assured Dr. Jekyll that Hyde was safe. Dr. Jekyll said he had burned the envelope, but there was no postmark.

6. What else did Mr. Utterson discover about the note when he talked to Poole?

   He found out that no messenger had come with the note, and it had not been delivered by mail.

7. Who was Mr. Guest? What did he discover? What was Mr. Utterson's conclusion?

   Mr. Guest was Mr. Utterson's head clerk. He was also a handwriting expert. He discovered that Mr. Hyde's writing strongly resembled Dr. Jekyll's writing. That discovery led Mr. Utterson to believe Dr. Jekyll had forged the note for the murderer.

8. Describe all of the changes in Dr. Jekyll after Mr. Hyde's disappearance. What did he say about seeing Dr. Lanyon again?

   For about two months it seemed that Dr. Jekyll was back to his old self. He entertained, and he looked much better. Then, suddenly, he stopped seeing people. In response to Mr. Utterson's letter about Dr. Lanyon, Dr. Jekyll agreed that the two must never meet again. Dr. Jekyll said he was going to lead a life of seclusion.

9. After a few nights of being refused entrance to see Dr. Jekyll, Mr. Utterson went to visit Dr. Lanyon. Summarize the visit, including what Mr. Utterson thought was wrong. What did Dr. Lanyon say about Dr. Jekyll? What later happened to Dr. Lanyon?

   Dr. Lanyon looked very ill, almost near death. Mr. Utterson thought he looked like he had some "deep-seated terror of the mind." Dr. Lanyon said he did not want to see or hear about Dr. Jekyll ever again. Dr. Lanyon died about three weeks later.

10. Describe the envelope Mr. Utterson receives. Tell who gave it to him, what it says, and what is inside.

    The envelope was from Dr. Lanyon. The outside said "Private: for the hands of G. J. Utterson Alone, and in case of his predecease, to be destroyed unread. " Inside was another envelope that said, "not to be opened until the death or disappearance of Dr. Henry Jekyll.

Incident at the Window; The Last Night; Dr. Lanyon's Narrative

1. Where did Mr. Utterson and Mr. Enfield go for their Sunday walk? Whom did they see? What happened? How did they react?

   They went past Mr. Hyde's door, and decided to go into the courtyard and try to see Dr. Jekyll. He was sitting in the window and they conversed for a few minutes. He said he could not come down, and did not want to invite them up, but agreed with Mr. Utterson to chat from where they were. Suddenly his face got "an expression of abject terror and despair." The two men left the courtyard. They were pale and had a look of horror in their eyes.

2. What did Poole think happened to Dr. Jekyll?
   He suspected some type of foul play, possibly Dr. Jekyll's murder.

3. Poole said Dr. Jekyll had been asking for something all week. How was he asking for it? What was it? What type did he want?
   He had been writing notes and throwing them on the steps. The notes instructed Poole to go to the wholesale chemists in town to buy a certain type of drug. The last letter asked the Messrs. Maw to "find him some of the old."

4. Whom and what did Poole, Bradshaw, and Mr. Utterson find when they broke the door down?
   They found Edward Hyde, dressed in clothes that were too big for him. However, the clothes would have fit the doctor. Mr. Hyde was dead. They also found piles of the white salt and other traces of chemical works. Mr. Utterson found an envelope in the doctor's handwriting that was addressed to him (Utterson.)

5. Summarize the note Dr. Lanyon received. Tell when he received it, what it said, and who had signed it.
   Dr. Lanyon received a note from Dr. Jekyll on January 9. In the note he asked Dr. Lanyon to take a cab to his (Dr. Jekyll's) house and take the fourth drawer from the top of the cabinet, with all of its contents. He was to take the drawer back to his own home and wait for a messenger from Dr. Jekyll. At midnight the messenger would come and Dr. Lanyon was to hand him the drawer.

6. Describe the messenger.
   The messenger was Mr. Hyde. His clothes looked much too big for him.

7. Retell, in order, the events at Dr. Lanyon's house.
   Mr. Hyde mixed the powder and red liquid, which changed to a dark purple, then watery green. Then he asked Dr. Lanyon if he (Hyde) should drink the potion there so that Dr. Lanyon could see the results, or if he should leave. Dr. Lanyon asked him to continue. Mr. Hyde drank the potion and changed into Dr. Jekyll. The two men talked after that for about an hour.

8. How did Dr. Lanyon say he felt after this meeting?
   He said his life was shaken, he could not sleep, and he was full of terror. He felt he would die soon.

<u>Henry Jekyll's Full Statement of the Case</u>
1. What did Henry Jekyll say his worst fault was? What was difficult about this fault?
   It was a "certain impatient gaiety of disposition." He found it bothersome to feel so light-hearted, because he wanted to appear serious to the public.

2. What did Dr. Jekyll do about his faults and irregularities?
   He hid them with a sense of shame.

3. In what direction did Henry Jekyll's scientific studies go, and why?
   His studies went in the direction of the mystic and transcendental. He studied the duality of man's nature.

4. Describe, in order, the process Dr. Jekyll went through when he prepared his tincture. Include the results.
   He bought the salt from a chemical wholesale company. He compounded the elements and drank the potion. He experienced racking pangs, grinding bones, nausea, and a horror of the spirit. Then he came to himself and felt younger and livelier. He knew he was more wicked. He was aware he was shorter. He became Mr. Hyde.

5. What was Dr. Jekyll's theory on Hyde's different size?
   He thought the evil side of his nature was less developed than the good.

6. Dr. Jekyll said he had two characters and two appearances. Describe and name each.
   Dr. Jekyll was still a compound of good and evil, but Mr. Hyde was totally evil.

7. At one point Dr. Jekyll said he no longer feared the gallows. What horror did bother him?
   It was the horror of being Hyde.

8. What started happening to Dr. Jekyll the day after he visited Dr. Lanyon?
   He started changing into Mr. Hyde and could only keep his form as Dr. Jekyll for about six hours without taking the drug. The pangs of transformation grew weaker.

9. How did Dr. Jekyll describe Mr. Hyde's feelings for him?
   Dr. Jekyll said Mr. Hyde despised him. He retreated to Dr. Jekyll's body because he feared the gallows, but he resented doing so.

10. What conclusion did Dr. Jekyll draw about the original powder?
    It had an impurity that made the potion effective.

MULTIPLE CHOICE STUDY/QUIZ QUESTIONS *Dr. Jekyll and Mr. Hyde*

<u>Story of the Door; Search for Mr. Hyde</u>

1. Who is being described? He was cold and never smiled. He was tall and lean. He tolerated others, and was more inclined to help than to reprove
   A. Mr. Utterson
   B. Dr. Jekyll
   C. Mr. Richard Enfield
   D. Poole

2. What did Mr. Utterson and Mr. Enfield see that reminded Mr. Enfield of an odd story?
   A. They saw a broken second story window.
   B. They saw a rotting tree trunk.
   C. They saw a blistered and distainted door.
   D. They saw a bent street sign.

3. Which of the following statements was **not** included in Mr. Enfield's story?
   A. Mr. Enfield ran after the man and brought him back.
   B. The family beat the man.
   C. The man gave the family a check signed by a well-known person.
   D. A little man trampled over a young girl and left her screaming on the ground.

4. True or False: Mr. Enfield called the house Black Mail House.
   A. True
   B. False

5. What was the name of the man in Mr. Enfield's story?
   A. Dr. Jekyll
   B. Mr. Albertson
   C. Dr. Lanyon
   D. Mr. Hyde

6. True or False: Mr. Enfield had charge of Dr. Jekyll's will.
   A. True
   B. False

7. Which phrase in Dr. Jekyll's will bothered his lawyer?
   A. Mr. Hyde was Dr. Jekyll's nephew and should receive a monthly allowance.
   B. Dr. Jekyll wanted to leave all of his possessions to Mr. Hyde.
   C. The lawyer was to do whatever Mr. Hyde wanted.
   D. If Dr. Jekyll disappeared for more than three months, Mr. Hyde should step into his shoes.

8. True or False: Dr. Lanyon disagreed with some of Dr. Jekyll's scientific ideas.
   A. True
   B. False

9. Which of these was **not** one of the feelings Mr. Utterson expressed for Mr. Hyde?
   A. pity
   B. disgust
   C. fear
   D. loathing

10. What did Mr. Utterson discover when he went to Dr. Jekyll's house?
    A. Mr. Hyde dined with Dr. Jekyll every night.
    B. Mr. Hyde came and went through the front door.
    C. Mr. Hyde had a key to the house.
    D. Mr. Hyde received a monthly allowance from Dr. Jekyll.

Dr. Jekyll Was Quite At Ease - Remarkable Incident of Dr. Lanyon

1. What did Mr. Utterson agree to do for Dr. Jekyll?
   A. He agreed to hold onto the will for one year.
   B. He agreed to find a house for Mr. Hyde.
   C. He agreed to invite Dr. Lanyon and Dr. Jekyll to a dinner together.
   D. He agreed to help Mr. Hyde if the doctor were no longer around.

2. True or False: Dr. Lanyon thought Dr. Jekyll's scientific theories were brilliant.
   A. True
   B. False

3. Which of the statements about the murder is **false?**
   A. A maid was looking out her window and saw the entire murder.
   B. Sir Danvers Carew, a Member of Parliament, was murdered near midnight.
   C. The murdered man was carrying an envelope addressed to Dr. Jekyll.
   D. The murder took place about a year after the previous chapter.

4. What did Mr. Utterson and Inspector Newcomen find at Mr. Hyde's house?
   A. They found Dr. Jekyll's cheque book.
   B. They found the murdered man's gold watch and chain.
   C. They found Mr. Hyde, asleep.
   D. They found the other half of the cane that was used in the murder.

5. True or False: The note assured Dr. Jekyll that Hyde was safe.
   A. True
   B. False

6. What else did Mr. Utterson discover about the note when he talked to Poole?
   A. Mr. Hyde had delivered the note in person.
   B. Poole had written it to cover for Dr. Jekyll.
   C. No messenger had come with the note
   D. It had been delivered in the early morning mail.

7. What did Mr. Guest discover?
   A. The fingerprints on the note belonged to Dr. Jekyll.
   B. He discovered that Mr. Hyde's writing strongly resembled Dr. Jekyll's writing.
   C. The note paper had traces of a poison on it.
   D. The ink was still wet, which meant the note had been written about an hour earlier.

8. True or False: Dr. Jekyll agreed that he and Dr. Lanyon must never meet again.
   A. True
   B. False

9. What happened to Dr. Lanyon?
    A. He left the country and was never heard from again.
    B. He renewed his friendship with Dr. Jekyll.
    C. He died a few weeks after Mr. Utterson's visit.
    D. He went insane and was committed to an asylum.

10. Which phrase completes the statement on the envelope? Private: for the hands of . . .
    A. Dr. Jekyll, and if he is not found, to be read by Mr. Hyde.
    B. Dr. Lanyon, to be read at the funeral of Dr. Jekyll.
    C. Poole, to be then delivered to Mr. Utterson.
    D. G. J. Utterson alone, and in case of his predecease, to be destroyed unread.

Incident at the Window; The Last Night; Dr. Lanyon's Narrative

1. True or False: While conversing with Dr. Jekyll, Mr. Utterson and Mr. Enfield watched the doctor's face get an expression of terror and despair.
    A. True
    B. False

2. Who suspected that Dr. Jekyll was the victim of foul play?
    A. Mr. Utterson
    B. Dr. Lanyon
    C. Poole
    D. Bradshaw

3. What had Dr. Jekyll had been asking for all week?
    A. He had been asking for Mr. Utterson to visit him.
    B. He had been asking for paper to write to Mr. Hyde.
    C. He had been asking for a lot of food to be brought to his laboratory.
    D. He had been asking for some of the old drug.

4. Which was **not** found when Poole, Bradshaw, and Mr. Utterson broke the door down?
    A. piles of white salt and other traces of chemicals
    B. Dr. Jekyll, alive but weak
    C. an envelope addressed to Mr. Utterson
    D. Mr. Hyde, dead

5. Whom did the clothes in the room fit?
    A. Mr. Hyde
    B. Poole
    C. Dr. Lanyon
    D. Dr. Jekyll

6. Who had received a note from Dr. Jekyll giving instructions?
    A. the housekeeper
    B. Poole
    C. Dr. Lanyon
    D. Inspector Newcomen

7. What did Dr. Jekyll want?
    A. his cheque book
    B. a certain cabinet drawer
    C. his clothes
    D. 1000 pounds in gold coins

8. True or False: The messenger was Mr. Utterson.
   A. True
   B. False

9. Which statement is true?
   A. Mr. Hyde drank the potion and changed into Dr. Jekyll.
   B. Dr. Jekyll drank the potion and changed into Mr. Hyde.

10. How did Dr. Lanyon say he felt after this?
    A. He was excited at the new scientific breakthrough.
    B. He was glad to get to know Dr. Jekyll better.
    C. He was relieved to get rid of Mr. Hyde.
    D. He was full of terror. He felt he would die soon.

Henry Jekyll's Full Statement of the Case

1. True or False: Dr. Jekyll found it bothersome to feel so light-hearted, because he wanted to appear serious to the public.
   A. True
   B. False

2. What did Dr. Jekyll do about his faults and irregularities?
   A. He talked to his minister about them.
   B. He busied himself with studies and good works.
   C. He worked to correct them.
   D. He hid them with a sense of shame.

3. Which is **not** one of the directions that Henry Jekyll's scientific studies took?
   A. the mystic
   B. man's inhumanity to man
   C. transcendental
   D. the duality of man's nature

4. List, in order, the process Dr. Jekyll went through when he prepared his tincture.
   A. He experienced racking pangs, grinding bones, nausea, and a horror of the spirit.
   B. He compounded the elements and drank the potion.
   C. He came to himself and felt younger and livelier. He knew he was more wicked.
   D. He bought the salt from a chemical wholesale company.

5. True or False: Dr. Jekyll thought the evil and good sides of his nature were the same size.
   A. True
   B. False

6. Which statement is true?
   A. Dr. Jekyll was all good, and Mr. Hyde was all evil.
   B. Dr. Jekyll and Mr. Hyde were both combinations of good and evil.
   C. Dr. Jekyll was all good, but Mr. Hyde was a compound of good and evil.
   D. Dr. Jekyll was still a compound of good and evil, but Mr. Hyde was totally evil.

7. What horror bothered Dr. Jekyll?
   A. waking up and living with his conscience
   B. being Hyde
   C. the realization that others might try his drug
   D. the gallows

8. What started happening to Dr. Jekyll the day after he visited Dr. Lanyon?
    A. He could only keep his form as Dr. Jekyll for about six hours without taking the drug.
    B. He ran out of the drug completely and was trapped as Mr. Hyde.
    C. He could not remember anything that had happened to him.
    D. He had an uncontrollable urge to kill all of his friends.

9. True or False: Mr. Hyde despised Dr. Jekyll.
    A. True
    B. False

10. What conclusion did Dr. Jekyll draw about the original powder?
    A. He had forgotten the original formula.
    B. The powder only worked once; then the drinker was immune to it.
    C. It had an impurity that made the potion effective.
    D. It was poisoned and was slowly killing him.

STUDENT ANSWER SHEET-MULTIPLE CHOICE/QUIZ QUESTIONS

Story of the Door; Search for Mr. Hyde

1.
2.
3.
4.
5.
6.
7.
8.
9.
10.

Dr. Jekyll Was Quite At Ease; The Carew Murder Case; Incident of the Letter; Remarkable Incident of Dr. Lanyon

1.
2.
3.
4.
5.
6.
7.
8.
9.
10.

Incident at the Window; The Last Night; Dr. Lanyon's Narrative

1.
2.
3.
4.
5.
6.
7.
8.
9.
10.

Henry Jekyll's Full Statement of the Case

1.
2.
3.
4.
5.
6.
7.
8.
9.
10.

ANSWER KEY-MULTIPLE CHOICE/QUIZ QUESTIONS

Story of the Door; Search for Mr. Hyde

1. A
2. C
3. B
4. A TRUE
5. D
6. B FALSE
7. D
8. A TRUE
9. A
10. C

Dr. Jekyll Was Quite At Ease; The Carew Murder Case; Incident of the Letter; Remarkable Incident of Dr. Lanyon

1. D
2. B FALSE
3. C
4. D
5. A TRUE
6. C
7. B
8. A TRUE
9. C
10. D

Incident at the Window; The Last Night; Dr. Lanyon's Narrative

1. A TRUE
2. C
3. D
4. B
5. D
6. C
7. B
8. B FALSE
9. A
10. D

Henry Jekyll's Full Statement of the Case

1. A TRUE
2. D
3. B
4. D, B, A, C
5. B FALSE
6. D
7. B
8. A
9. A TRUE
10. C

PREREADING VOCABULARY WORKSHEETS

VOCABULARY WORKSHEETS *Dr. Jekyll & Mr. Hyde*

<u>Story of the Door, Search for Mr. Hyde</u>

Part I: Using Prior Knowledge and Context Clues

Below are the sentences in which the vocabulary words appear in the text. Read the sentence. Use any clues you can find in the sentence combined with your prior knowledge, and write what you think the underlined words mean on the lines provided.

1. At friendly meetings, and when the wine was to his taste, something ***eminently*** human beaconed from his eye.

   _____

2. He was ***austere*** with himself; drank gin when he was alone, to mortify a taste for vintages.

   _____

3. . . . and in any extremity inclined to help rather than to ***reprove***.

   _____

4. That evening Mr. Utterson came home to his bachelor house in ***sombre*** spirits and sat down to dinner without relish.

   _____

5. It was worse when it began to be clothed upon with ***detestable*** attributes.

   _____

6. "Did you ever come across a ***protégé*** of his--one Hyde?" he asked.

   _____

7. Then he began slowly to mount the street, pausing every step or two and putting his hand to his brow like a man in mental ***perplexity***.

   _____

8. "Your master seems to ***repose*** a great deal of trust in that young man, Poole," resumed the other musingly.

   _____

Dr. Jekyll & Mr. Hyde Vocabulary Worksheets Page 2

9. Ay, it must be that; the ghost of some old sin, the cancer of some concealed disgrace; punishment coming, pede clauso, years after memory has forgotten and self-love **_condoned_** the fault."

_____

10. And the lawyer, scared by the thought, brooded awhile on is own past, groping in all the corners of memory, lest by chance some Jack-in-the- Box of an old **_iniquity_** should leap to light there.

_____

Part II: Determining the Meaning   Match the vocabulary words to their dictionary definitions.

1. eminently
2. austere
3. reprove
4. sombre
5. detestable
6. protégé
7. perplexity
8. repose
9. condoned
10. iniquity

A. strict; stern
B. confusion; puzzlement
C. gloom; depressing
D. overlooked; forgiven
E. outstanding
F. hateful; nasty
G. wickedness; injustice
H. a person under the support of a patron
I. rebuke; scold
J. to place trust in

Dr. Jekyll & Mr. Hyde Vocabulary Worksheets Page 3

Dr. Jekyll Was Quite at Ease, The Carew Murder Case; Incident of the Letter, Remarkable Incident of Dr. Lanyon

Part I: Using Prior Knowledge and Context Clues

Below are the sentences in which the vocabulary words appear in the text. Read the sentence. Use any clues you can find in the sentence combined with your prior knowledge, and write what you think the underlined words mean on the lines provided.

1. They liked to sit awhile in his **_unobtrusive_** company, practising for solitude, sobering their minds in the man's rich silence after the expense and strain of gaiety.

   _____

2. "It can make no change. You do not understand my position," returned the doctor, with a certain **_incoherency_** of manner.

   _____

3. When they had come within speech (which was just under the maid's eyes) the older man bowed and **_accosted_** the other with a very pretty manner of politeness.

   _____

4. The stick with which the deed had been done, although it was of some rare and very tough and heavy wood, had broken in the middle under the stress of this **_insensate_** cruelty.

   _____

5. Mr. Utterson beheld a marvelous number of degrees and hues of twilight; for here it would be dark like the back-end of evening; and there would be a glow of a rich, lurid brown, like the light of some strange **_conflagration_**; and here, for a moment, the fog would be quite broken up. . .

   _____

6. A flash of **_odious_** joy appeared upon the woman's face. "Ah!" said she, "he is in trouble! What has he done?"

   _____

Dr. Jekyll & Mr. Hyde Vocabulary Worksheets Page 4

7. From these embers the inspector ***disinterred*** the butt end of a green cheque book, which had resisted the action of the fire. . .

_____

8. . . . and he eyed the dingy, windowless structure with curiosity, and gazed round with a distasteful sense of strangeness as he crossed the theatre, once crowded with eager students and not lying ***gaunt*** and silent, the tables laden wit chemical apparatus. . .

_____

9. Utterson ***ruminated*** awhile; he was surprised at this friend's selfishness, and yet relieved by it.

_____

10. "One moment. I thank you, sir," and the clerk laid the two sheets of paper alongside and ***sedulously*** compared their contents.

_____

Part II: Determining the Meaning   Match the vocabulary words to their dictionary definitions.

1. unobtrusive
2. incoherency
3. accosted
4. insensate
5. conflagration
6. odious
7. disinterred
8. gaunt
9. ruminated
10. sedulously

A. a great fire
B. spoke to first
C. diligently
D. dug up
E. pondered; reflected over and over
F. unable to express one's thoughts clearly
G. lean and angular
H. hateful
I. not noticeable
J. without feeling

Dr. Jekyll & Mr. Hyde Vocabulary Worksheets Page 5

Incident at the Window, The Last Night, Dr. Lanyon's Narrative
Part I: Using Prior Knowledge and Context Clues
Below are the sentences in which the vocabulary words appear in the text. Read the sentence. Use any clues you can find in the sentence combined with your prior knowledge, and write what you think the underlined words mean on the lines provided.

1. The middle one of the three windows was half-way open; and sitting close behind it, taking the air with an infinite sadness of ***mien***, like some disconsolate prisoner, Utterson saw Dr. Jekyll.

   _____

2. The middle one of the three windows was half-way open; and sitting close behind it, taking the air with an infinite sadness of mien, like some ***disconsolate*** prisoner, Utterson say Dr. Jekyll.

   _____

3. But the words were hardly uttered, before the smile was struck out of his face and succeeded by an expression of such ***abject*** terror and despair, as froze the very blood of the two gentlemen below.

   _____

4. He could have wished it otherwise; never in his life had he been conscious of so sharp a wish to see and touch his fellow-creatures; for struggle as he might, there was borne in upon his mind a crushing anticipation of ***calamity.***

   _____

5. Poole said to her, with a ferocity of accent that testified to his own jangled nerves; and indeed, when the girl had so suddenly raised the note of her ***lamentation***, they had all started and turned towards the inner door with faces of dreadful expectation.

   _____

6. "There is my explanation; it is sad enough, Poole, ay, and appalling to consider; but it is plain and natural, hangs well together, and delivers us from all ***exorbitant*** alarms."

   _____

Dr. Jekyll & Mr. Hyde Vocabulary Worksheets Page 6

7. The phial, to which I next turned my attention, night have been about half full of a blood-red liquor, which was highly pungent to the sense of smell and seemed to me to contain phosphorous and some ***volatile*** ether.

_____

8. This bore some resemblance to ***incipient*** rigour, and was accompanied by a marked sinking of the pulse.

_____

9. My visitor, who had watched these metamorphoses with a keen eye, smiled, set down the glass upon the table, and then turned and looked upon me with an air of ***scrutiny***.

_____

10. "Sir," said I, affecting a coolness that I was far from truly possessing, "you speak ***enigmas***, and you will perhaps not wonder that I hear you with no very strong impression of belief."

_____

Part II: Determining the Meaning   Match the vocabulary words to their dictionary definitions.

1. mien   A. disaster
2. disconsolate   B. close examination
3. abject   C. behavior; bearing
4. calamity   D. beginning; in an early stage
5. lamentation   E. grieving; expressing sorrow
6. exorbitant   F. wretched; lacking pride
7. volatile   G. excessive
8. incipient   H. sad
9. scrutiny   I. puzzles
10. enigmas   J. evaporating rapidly

Dr. Jekyll & Mr. Hyde Vocabulary Worksheets Page 7

<u>Henry Jekyll's Full Statement of the Case</u>
Part I: Using Prior Knowledge and Context Clues
Below are the sentences in which the vocabulary words appear in the text. Read the sentence. Use any clues you can find in the sentence combined with your prior knowledge, and write what you think the underlined words mean on the lines provided.

1. I was born in the year 18-- to a large fortune, ***endowed*** besides with excellent parts, inclined by nature to industry, fond of the respect of the wise and good among my fellowmen. . .

   _____

2. And indeed the worst of my faults was a certain impatient gaiety of disposition, such as has made the happiness of many, but such as I found it hard to reconcile with my ***imperious*** desire to carry my head high, and wear a more than commonly grave countenance before the public.

   _____

3. In this case, I was driven to reflect deeply and ***inveterately*** on that hard law of life, which lies at the root of religion and is one of the most plentiful springs of distress.

   _____

4. And it chanced that the direction of my scientific studies, which led wholly towards the mystic and the transcendental, reacted and shed a strong light on this consciousness of the ***perennial*** war among my members.

   _____

5. Others will follow, others will outstrip me on the same lines; and I hazard the guess that man will be ultimately known for a mere polity of ***multifarious***, incongruous and independent denizens.

   _____

6. Others will follow, others will outstrip me on the same lines; and I hazard the guess that man will be ultimately known for a mere polity of multifarious, ***incongruous*** and independent denizens.

   _____

Dr. Jekyll & Mr. Hyde Vocabulary Worksheets Page 8

7. The evil side of my nature, to which I had now transferred the stamping ***efficacy***, was less robust and less developed than the good which I had just deposed.

   _____

8. Even at that time, I had not conquered my ***aversions*** to the dryness of a life of study.

   _____

9. I next drew up that will to which you so much objected; so that if anything befell me in the person of Dr. Jekyll, I could enter on that of Mr. Hyde without ***pecuniary*** loss.

   _____

10. There comes an end to all things; the most ***capacious*** measure is filled at last; and this brief condescension to my evil finally destroyed the balance of my soul.

    _____

Part II: Determining the Meaning   Match the vocabulary words to their dictionary definitions.

1. endowed
2. imperious
3. inveterately
4. perennial
5. multifarious
6. incongruous
7. efficacy
8. aversions
9. pecuniary
10. capacious

A. domineering; arrogant
B. power to produce the desired effect
C. varied; greatly diversified
D. relating to money
E. supplied with a quality
F. deep rooted; habitually
G. absurd; incompatible
H. large
I. continuing; recurring
J. firm dislike

ANSWER SHEET PREREADING VOCABULARY *Jekyll & Hyde*

Directions: Fill in the correct chapter number. Use as many of the lines as needed.

Chapter ___		Chapter ___	
Part 1	Pt.2	Part 1	Pt.2
1. _____	___	1. _____	___
2. _____	___	2. _____	___
3. _____	___	3. _____	___
4. _____	___	4. _____	___
5. _____	___	5. _____	___
6. _____	___	6. _____	___
7. _____	___	7. _____	___
8. _____	___	8. _____	___
9. _____	___	9. _____	___
10. _____	___	10. _____	___

Chapter ___		Chapter ___	
Part 1	Pt.2	Part 1	Pt.2
1. _____	___	1. _____	___
2. _____	___	2. _____	___
3. _____	___	3. _____	___
4. _____	___	4. _____	___
5. _____	___	5. _____	___
6. _____	___	6. _____	___
7. _____	___	7. _____	___
8. _____	___	8. _____	___
9. _____	___	9. _____	___
10. _____	___	10. _____	___

ANSWER KEY-PREREADING VOCABULARY WORKSHEETS *Jekyll & Hyde*

Story of the Door, Search for Mr. Hyde

1. E
2. A
3. I
4. C
5. F
6. H
7. B
8. J
9. D
10. G

Dr. Jekyll Was Quite at Ease, The Carew Murder Case; Incident of the Letter, Remarkable Incident of Dr. Lanyon

1. I
2. F
3. B
4. J
5. A
6. H
7. D
8. G
9. E
10. C

Incident at the Window, The Last Night, Dr. Lanyon's Narrative

1. C
2. H
3. F
4. A
5. E
6. G
7. J
8. D
9. B
10. I

Henry Jekyll's Full Statement of the Case

1. E
2. A
3. F
4. I
5. C
6. G
7. B
8. J
9. D
10. H

ADDITIONAL VOCABULARY *Jekyll & Hyde*

To the Teacher: Although the following words will not be tested, you may want to go over them with your students. A contextual sentence and definition is provided for each word.

Story of the Door

1. Mr. Utterson the lawyer was a man of a rugged ***countenance*** that was never lighted by a
2. smile; cold, scanty and embarrassed in ***discourse*** . . .
    countenance: face; facial expression
    discourse: talk; conversation

3. And to such as these, so long as they came about his chambers, he never marked a shade of change in his ***demeanour***.
    demeanour: (demeanor) manner; behavior

4. . . . his affections, like ivy, were the growth of time, they implied no ***aptness*** in the object.
    aptness: qualification; expertise

5. The inhabitants were all doing well, it seemed, and all ***emulously*** hoping to do better still, and
6. laying out the surplus of their gains in ***coquetry*** . . .
    emulously: eagerly trying to equal or surpass another
    coquetry: flirtation

7. It was two storeys high; showed no window. Nothing but a door on the lower storey and a
8. blind forehead of discoloured wall on the upper; and bore in every feature, the marks of ***prolonged*** and ***sordid*** negligence.
    prolonged: lengthy; drawn out
    sordid: filthy; squalid

9. It wasn't like a man; it was like some damned ***Juggernaut***.
    Juggernaut: An overwhelming, advancing force that crushes or seems to crush everything in its path

10. He was the usual cut and dry ***apothecary***, of no particular age and colour, with a strong Edinburgh accent, and about as emotional as a bagpipe.
    apothecary: one who prepares and sells drugs and other medicines; a pharmacist

11. I took the liberty of pointing out to my gentleman that the whole business looked ***apocryphal***, and that a man does not, in real life, walk into a cellar door at four in the morning and come out with another man's cheque for close upon a hundred pounds.
    apocryphal: of doubtful authenticity

12. "I think you might have warned me," returned the other with a touch of ***sullenness***.
    sullenness: resentment; sulkiness

Additional Vocabulary *Jekyll & Hyde* Page 2

13. "But I have been ***pedantically*** exact, as you call it."
    pedantically: a narrow focus on the trivial aspects of learning

Search for Mr. Hyde

1. That evening Mr. Utterson came home to his bachelor house in sombre spirits and sat down to dinner without ***relish***.
    relish: an appetite

2. The will was a ***holograph***, for Mr. Utterson, though he took charge of tit now that it was made, had refused to lend the least assistance in the making of it;
    holograph: A document written wholly in the handwriting of the person whose signature it bears

3. "Such unscientific ***balderdash***," added the doctor, flushing suddenly purple, "would have
4. estranged ***Damon and Pythias***."

    balderdash: nonsense
    Damon and Pythias Damon was a mythological figure who, out of devotion, pledged his life as a guarantee that his condemned friend Pythias would return to face execution. Both were subsequently pardoned

5. He was small and plainly dressed, and the look of him, even at that distance, went somehow strongly against the watcher's ***inclination***.
    inclination: the disposition to prefer, or favor one thing rather than another

6. Something ***troglodytic***, shall we say?
    troglodytic: having to do with cave men; an anthropoid ape, such as a gorilla or chimp

7. He was wild when he was young; a long time ago to be sure, but in the law of God, there is no ***statute of limitations***.
    statute of limitations : a law setting a time limit on legal actions

Dr. Jekyll Was Quite At Ease

1. A ***fortnight*** later, by excellent good fortune, the doctor gave one of his pleasant dinners to
2. some five or six old ***cronies***, all intelligent, reputable men . . .
    fortnight : two weeks; fourteen days
    cronies: long time close friends

Additional Vocabulary *Jekyll & Hyde* Page 3

3. "I never saw a man so distressed as you were by my will; unless it were that hide-bound
4. ***pedant***, Lanyon, at what he called my scientific ***heresies***."
    pedant: one who pays undue attention to book learning and formal rules
    heresies: controversial or unusual opinions

5. Utterson heaved an ***irrepressible*** sigh.
    irrepressible: difficult or impossible to control or restrain

The Carew Murder Case
1. Mr. Utterson had already ***quailed*** at the name of Hyde. . .
    quailed: shrunk back in fear

2. It was by this time about nine in the morning, and the first fog of the season. A great chocolate-colored ***pall*** lowered over the heaven. . .
    pall: a covering

3. The dismal quarter of Soho seen under these changing glimpses, with its muddy ways, and ***slatternly*** passengers, and its lamps, which had never been extinguished. . .
    slatternly: untidy; dirty

Incident of the Letter
1. The fog still slept on the wing above the drowned city, where the lamps glimmered like ***carbuncles.*** . .
    carbuncles: deep red garnets; precious red stones

2. "Rather ***quaint***," said Utterson.
    quaint: odd, in an old fashioned way

Remarkable Incident of Dr. Lanyon
1. As soon as he got home, Utterson sat down and wrote to Jekyll, complaining of his exclusion
2. from the house, and asking the cause of this unhappy break with Lanyon; and the next day brought him a long answer, often ***pathetically*** worded, and sometimes darkly mysterious in ***drift***.
    pathetically: arousing sympathy or compassion
    drift: general meaning

3. A great curiosity came on the trustee, to disregard the ***prohibition*** and dive at once to the bottom of these mysteries. . .
    prohibition: forbidding something

Additional Vocabulary *Jekyll & Hyde* Page 4

4. . . . but professional honour and faith to his dead friend were ***stringent*** obligations
    stringent: strict; binding

5. It is one thing to ***mortify*** curiosity, another to conquer it. . .
    mortify: to discipline by self-denial

The Last Night

1. "What, what? Are you all here?" said the lawyer ***peevishly***.
    peevishly: in an ill-tempered way

2. "Suppose it were as you suppose, supposing Dr. Jekyll to have been--well, murdered, what could ***induce*** the murderer to stay?"
    induce: persuade

3. "Why, you and me, sir," was the ***undaunted*** reply.
    undaunted: courageous; not discouraged

4. "Meanwhile, lest anything should really be amiss, or any ***malefactor*** seek to escape by the back, you and the boy must go round the corner with a pair of good sticks and take your post at the laboratory door."
    malefactor: wrongdoer; lawbreaker

5. . . . and they drew near with ***bated*** breath to where that patient foot was still going up and down, up and down in the quiet of the night.
    bated: moderate; slowed down

6. . . and by the crushed ***phial*** in the hand and the strong smell of kernels that hung upon the air, Utterson knew that he was looking on the body of a self-destroyer.
    phial: vial; a small container for liquids

Dr. Lanyon's Narrative

1. In my extreme distress of mind, I have a ***morbid*** fear of misdirecting you. . .
    morbid: preoccupied with unwholesome thoughts or feelings

2. The less I understood of this ***farrago***, the less I wan in a position to judge of its importance. . .
    farrago: an assortment or mixture

3. He told me "yes" by a ***constrained*** gesture. . .
    constrained: held back; confined

Additional Vocabulary *Jekyll & Hyde* Page 5

4. I was struck besides with the shocking expression of his face, with his remarkable
5. combination of great muscular activity and great apparent ***debility*** of ***constitution*** . . .
   debility: delicacy; fragility
   constitution: health

6. As for the moral ***turpitude*** that man unveiled to me, even with tears of penitence, I cannot, even in memory, dwell on it without a start of horror.
   turpitude: depravity; evil

Henry Jekyll's Full Statement of the Case

1. I began to perceive more deeply than it has eer yet been stated, the trembling immateriality, the mistlike ***transience***, of this seemingly so solid body in which we walk attired.
   transience: passing; not lasting long

2. . . . and late one night, I compounded the elements, watched them boil and smoke together in the glass, and when the ***ebullition*** had subsided, with a strong glow of courage, drank off the potion.
   ebullition: seething; bubbling

3. . . . and engaged as a housekeeper a creature whom I knew to be silent and ***unscrupulous***.
   unscrupulous: dishonest; deceitful

4. I was often plunged into a kind of wonder at my ***vicarious*** depravity.
   vicarious: felt as if one were taking part in the experience of another

5. I was often plunged into a kind of wonder at my vicarious ***depravity***.
   depravity: moral corruptness

6. . . . but the situation was apart from ordinary laws, and ***insidiously*** relaxed the grasp of conscience.
   insidiously: spreading in a harmful manner

DAILY LESSON PLANS

LESSON ONE

Objectives
    1. to preview the unit on *The Strange Case of Dr. Jekyll and Mr. Hyde*
    2. To receive books and other related materials
    3. To relate prior knowledge to the new material
    4. To become familiar with the nonfiction writing assignment
    5. To practice writing to inform
    6. To learn to do library research

Activity 1
Note to the Teacher: Most of the students will probably have heard of Jekyll and Hyde, although they have not read the book. Some of their information may be inaccurate. It will be important during this activity not to correct their inaccurate information and reveal the climax of the novel.

Before class begins, put pictures of 19th century England, especially London, on a bulletin board. You may also want to play some music to get students in the mood of the novel.

Do a group KWL sheet with the students (form included). Write the phrases "Dr. Jekyll" and "Mr. Hyde" on the board. Show any pictures of Jekyll and Hyde that you may have. Ask students what they know about Dr. Jekyll and Mr. Hyde. Put this information in the K column (What I Know). Ask students what they want to find out from reading the book and record that in the W column (What I Want To Find Out). Keep the sheet and refer back to it after reading the book. Complete the L column (What I Learned) at that time.

Activity 2
Tell students *The Strange Case of Dr. Jekyll and Mr. Hyde* is a mystery story. Encourage them to talk about other mysteries they have read, or mystery television shows or movies they have seen. Discuss the methods the authors use to plant clues in the story. Remind students to look for clues as they are reading, and to try to solve the mystery before the author reveals it.

Activity 3
Distribute the materials students will use in this unit. Explain in detail how students are to use these materials.

    Study Guides Students should preview the study guide questions before each reading assignment to get a feeling for what events and ideas are important in that section. After reading the section, students will (as a class or individually) answer the questions to review the important events and ideas from that section of the book. Students should keep the study guides as study materials for the unit test.

Reading Assignment Sheet You need to fill in the reading assignment sheet to let students know when their reading has to be completed. You can either write the assignment sheet on a side blackboard or bulletin board and leave it there for students to see each day, or you can "ditto" copies for each student to have. In either case, you should advise students to become very familiar with the reading assignments so they know what is expected of them.

Unit Outline You may find it helpful to distribute copies of the Unit Outline to your students so they can keep track of upcoming lessons and assignments. You may also want to post a copy of the Unit Outline on a bulletin board and cross off each lesson as you complete it.

Extra Activities Center The unit resource portion of this unit contains suggestions for a library of related books and articles in your classroom as well as crossword and word search puzzles. Make an extra activities center in your room where you will keep these materials for students to use. (Bring the books and articles in from the library and keep several copies of the puzzles on hand.) Explain to students that these materials are available for students to use when they finish reading assignment or other class work early.

Books Each school has its own rules and regulations regarding student use of school books. Advise students of the procedures that are normal for your school.

Notebook or Unit Folder   you may want the students to keep all of their worksheets, notes, and other papers for the unit together in a binder or notebook. During the first class meeting, tell them how you want them to arrange the folder. Make divider pages for vocabulary worksheets, prereading study guide questions, review activities, notes, and tests. You may want to give a grade for accuracy in keeping the folder.

Activity #4
Distribute copies of the Nonfiction Assignment Sheet and go over it in detail with the students. Explain to students that they each are to read at least one nonfiction piece, write a report about it, and fill in the Nonfiction Assignment Sheet. The report will count as one of the three unit writing assignments, writing to inform. They will also present their information to the class in the form of an oral report during Lesson 17. The nonfiction piece could be a book, a magazine article, or information from an encyclopedia or the Internet. Also consider letting students watch an educational television show or video, such as a documentary. Give them the due date for the assignment (Lesson 7 for the writing assignment, Lesson 15 for the Nonfiction Assignment Sheet and Oral Report.)

Encourage students to research topics that are related to the novel. Some suggestions are: social conditions in Victorian England, the life of Robert Louis Stevenson, the class system in England, treatment of the mentally ill in the 19th century and the present time, research on multiple personalities, schizophrenia and other mental disorders, man's duality, the nature of good and evil. You may want to make this a partner or small group project.

Activity 5
Distribute copies of Writing Assignment 1. Go over the assignment in detail with the students. Tell them they will have the remainder of the class period to begin working on the assignment. Give the due date for the completed assignment. It should be a few days before the writing conferences, which are scheduled for Lesson 9.

Activity 6
Distribute copies of the Writing Evaluation Form. Explain to students that during Lesson 9 you will be holding individual writing conferences about this writing assignment. Make sure students are familiar with the criteria on the Writing Evaluation Form.

Follow-Up After you have graded the assignments, have a writing conference with each student. This Unit Plan schedules one in Lesson 9. After the writing conference, allow students to revise their papers using your suggestions to complete the revisions. Grade the revisions on an A-C-E scale: A = all revisions done well; C = some revisions made; E few or no revisions made. This will speed your grading time and still give some credit for students' efforts.

WRITING ASSIGNMENT 1 *Dr. Jekyll and Mr Hyde*

PROMPT

You are reading about Dr. Jekyll and Mr. Hyde. The setting for the story is London, sometime in the 1800s. Although the exact date is not given, the story was originally published in 1886. The descriptions are those of typical 19th century life. Choose a topic related to the story, learn more about it, and write a composition about what you have learned. Some suggested topics are: social conditions in Victorian era England, the moral ideas prevalent in Victorian England, the life of Robert Louis Stevenson, the class system in England, treatment of the mentally ill in the 19th century and today, research on multiple personalities, schizophrenia and other mental disorders, man's duality, or the nature of good and evil.

PREWRITING

Go to the library and find as many sources as you can on the topic you have chosen. Look for encyclopedias, books, magazine articles, videos, and Internet sources. You may want to interview an expert on the topic of your choice.

Think of questions you have about your topic. Write each one on a separate index card. Then, read to find the answers, and write the answers on your cards. Also take notes on interesting and important facts, even if you did not have questions directly related to them. Put each fact on a separate card. Make sure to cite your references. That means to write down the source and the page number for each one. Arrange your note cards in the order you want to use for your composition. Number them, perhaps in the upper right-hand corner. Read through them to make sure they make sense in that order. Rearrange as necessary.

DRAFTING

Introduce your topic in the first paragraph. Tell why you chose it and give a preview of what the rest of the paper will be about. Then write several paragraphs about the topic. Each paragraph should have a main idea and supporting details. Your last paragraph should summarize the information in the report.

PEER CONFERENCE/REVISING

When you finish the rough draft, ask another student to look at it. You may want to give the student your note cards so he/she can double check to see that you have included all the information you intended to include. After reading, he or she should tell you what was best about your report, which parts were difficult to understand or to follow, and ways in which your composition could be improved. Reread your report considering your critic's comments and make the corrections you think are necessary.

PROOFREADING/EDITING

Do a final proofreading of your report, double-checking your grammar, spelling, organization, and the clarity of your ideas.

NONFICTION ASSIGNMENT SHEET - *Jekyll and Hyde*

(To be completed after reading the required nonfiction article)

Name_____Date_____Class_____

Title of Nonfiction Read_____

Written By_____Publication Date_____

I. Factual Summary: Write a short summary of the piece you read.

II. Vocabulary:
 1. With which vocabulary words in the piece did you encounter some degree of difficulty?

 2. How did you resolve your lack of understanding of these words?

III. Interpretation: What was the main point the author wanted you to get from reading his/her work?

IV. Criticism:
 1. With which points of the piece did you agree or find easy to accept? Why?

 2. With which points of the piece did you disagree or find difficult to believe? Why?

V. Personal Response: What do you think about this piece? OR How does this piece influence your ideas?

WRITING EVALUATION FORM - *Dr. Jekyll and Mr. Hyde*

Name_____ Date_____ Class_____

Writing Assignment #1 for *Things Fall Apart*

Circle One For Each Item:

Introduction	excellent	good	fair	poor
Body Paragraphs_____	excellent	good	fair	poor
Summary_____	excellent	good	fair	poor
Grammar_____	excellent	good	fair	poor (errors noted)
Spelling_____	excellent	good	fair	poor (errors noted)
Punctuation_____	excellent	good	fair	poor (errors noted)
Legibility_____	excellent	good	fair	poor (errors noted)

Strengths:

Weaknesses:

Comments/Suggestions:

KWL *Dr. Jekyll & Mr. Hyde*

Directions: Before reading, think about what you already know about Robert Louis Stevenson's *Dr. Jekyll and Mr. Hyde*. Write the information in the K column. Think about what you would like to find out from reading the book. Write your questions in the W column. After you have read the book, use the L column to write the answers to your questions from the W column, and anything else you remember from the book.

K	W	L

LESSON TWO

Objectives
1. To understand the concept of theme in the novel
2. To complete the prereading vocabulary work for "Story of the Door" and "Search for Mr. Hyde"
3. To preview the study guide questions for "Story of the Door" and "Search for Mr. Hyde"
4. To read "Story of the Door" and "Search for Mr. Hyde"

Activity 1 Mini-Lesson Theme
Put the word **theme** on the board and ask student to tell what they think it means. Tell students that theme is the point the writer makes in the story. It related to a human truth or problem. The characters' emotions and values are involved. In an explicit theme, the meaning is stated clearly in the story. In an implicit theme, the meaning is suggested by the characters' thoughts, actions, and dialog. One main theme in Dickens' *Oliver Twist* is the poor treatment of children in England in the 19th century. An explicit theme in *Charlotte's Web* by E. B. White is friendship. A more implicit theme is that friends do things for each other. Tell students they will be discussing the themes of *The Strange Case of Dr. Jekyll and Mr. Hyde* both in their journals (Lesson 3) and during the Unit Review (Lesson 13).

Activity2
Work through the prereading vocabulary worksheet for "Story of the Door" and "Search for Mr. Hyde" with the students. Tell them they will have a sheet like this to complete before reading each section of the book.

Activity 3
Show students how to preview the study questions for "Story of the Door" and "Search for Mr. Hyde." Encourage students to predict what they think answers might be, to write down their predictions, and to compare these with their answers after reading the chapters. Tell them to bring the completed answers to the next class meeting.

Activity 4
Read "Story of the Door" aloud to students to set the mood for the novel. Then invite willing students to read aloud to the rest of the class. Students with some acting ability may enjoy the challenge of reading aloud using a British accent. If students do not complete the reading in class, assign it to be completed before the next class meeting.

LESSON THREE

Objectives
> 1. To discuss the main themes and events in "Story of the Door" and "Search for Mr. Hyde
> 2. To begin a sketchbook-journal (writing assignment 2)

Activity 1

Discuss the answers to the Study Guide questions for "Story of the Door" and "Search for Mr. Hyde" in detail. Write the answers on the board (or make transparencies of your answer key for the overhead projector) so students can have the correct answers for study purposes. Encourage students to take notes. If the students own their books, have them use high lighter pens to mark important passages and the answers to the study questions. it is a good practice in public speaking and leadership skills for individual students to take charge of leading the discussion of the study questions. Perhaps a different student could go to the front of the class and lead the discussion each day that the study questions are discussed during this unit. The teacher should guide the discussion when appropriate and be sure to fill in any gaps the students leave.

Activity 2

Tell students they will be keeping a sketchbook-journal as Writing Assignment 2. Explain that a sketchbook-journal is a combination of sketches about and written responses to the story. They will be required to make an entry for each chapter in the novel. Students can sketch memorable scenes from the chapters, or paste in magazine pictures or clip art images that remind them of events in the chapter. The written entries should focus on each student's response to the literature and should not merely be a plot summary. They should include comments about their thoughts and feelings while reading, any questions they have, and predictions for the next chapter. it is up to the individual teacher to decide how to grade or respond to the journals and whether or not to have students share them with the class or keep them private.

LESSON FOUR

Objectives
> 1. To complete the prereading vocabulary worksheet for "Dr. Jekyll Was Quite At Ease," "The Carew Murder Case," "Incident of the Letter," and "Remarkable Incident of Dr. Lanyon"
> 2. To preview the study questions for these chapters
> 3. To read these chapters
> 4. To read aloud for evaluation

Activity 1

Give students about ten minutes to go over the prereading vocabulary worksheets and preview the study questions.

Activity 2

Tell students their oral reading ability will be evaluated. Show them copies of the Oral Reading Evaluation Form and discuss it with them. Model correct intonation and expression by reading the first few paragraphs of "Dr. Jekyll Was Quite At Ease" aloud. Call on students to read a few paragraphs aloud. Encourage the other students to follow along silently in their books. If you have a student who is unwilling or unable to read in front of the group, make arrangements to do his or her evaluation privately at another time.

WRITING ASSIGNMENT 2 *Dr. Jekyll and Mr. Hyde*

PROMPT

For this unit, you will be asked to keep a sketchbook-journal. This is a combination of sketches about and written responses to a story. You will be required to make an entry for each chapter in the novel.

First decide on the format for your sketchbook-journal. Spend some time decorating your cover and setting up the book. Make sure to include the title of each chapter and the page numbers in your copy of the book. Also date each entry.

You can sketch memorable scenes from the chapters, paste in magazine pictures, or use computer clip art. Even if you do not consider yourself a good artist, try to make some sketches. Use colors that remind you of the mood of the story. You may want to take photographs and put them in the sketchbook-journal.

The written entries should focus on your response to the literature and should not merely be chapter summaries. They should include comments about your thoughts and feelings while reading, any questions you have, and predictions about the next chapter. Try to write at least one page for each entry.

Here are some suggestions for the types of entries you may want to make:

CHECK YOUR UNDERSTANDING	Explain how the story is making sense to you. Give examples and note page numbers. Establish the setting, mood, point of view, and character relationships. Discuss the stated themes.
MAKE INFERENCES	Explain your thoughts about the feelings and motives of the characters. Discuss the implied themes.
MAKE AND REVISE PREDICTIONS	At the end of each chapter, make a prediction about what you think will happen next. After you read, go back and check your predictions. Tell if you had to revise them, and why.
ASK QUESTIONS	Ask questions about scenes or events that are confusing. Record the answers if you discuss the questions in class or if you later find the answer in the novel.
GIVE YOUR OPINION	Give your opinion about the literary quality of the work. Discuss the author's style, use of language, and use of literary devices. Tell why you do or do not like the story. Tell how you feel while reading the chapters. Compare the book with others you have read.
MAKE CONNECTIONS	Think about ways the characters and events relate to your own life and experiences. Put yourself in a character's place and discuss how you would think or feel in that situation. Try this from the point of view of the main character and a few of the minor ones.
MAKE RECOMMENDATIONS	Tell what you think the characters should do or say. Tell how you would end the story or what you think might happen next.

ORAL READING EVALUATION - *Jekyll and Hyde*

Name_____Class_____Date_____

SKILL	EXCELLENT	GOOD	AVERAGE	FAIR	POOR
Fluency	5	4	3	2	1
Clarity	5	4	3	2	1
Audibility	5	4	3	2	1
Pronunciation	5	4	3	2	1
_____	5	4	3	2	1
_____	5	4	3	2	1

Total_____Grade_____

Comments:

LESSON FIVE

Objectives
> 1. To review the main ideas and events in "Dr. Jekyll Was Quite At Ease," "The Carew Murder Case," "Incident of the Letter," and "Remarkable Incident of Dr. Lanyon"
> 2. To identify examples of figurative language in the novel

Activity 1

Give each student four 1" x 2" strips of colored paper or index cards–one blue, one yellow, one green, one pink. Have tem put a large letter A on the blue paper, B on the yellow, C on the green and D on the pink. Distribute copies of the Multiple Choice Study/Quiz Questions for the chapters named above. Ask students to read the first question and hold up the colored paper for the correct answer. Have them mark the correct answer on their worksheets. Continue in this way for the entire quiz.

Activity 2 Mini-Lesson: Figures of Speech

Figures of speech are literary devices that give the writer a non-literal way to describe the images and events. Use the following chart to give examples of the different figures of speech. Then write "His affections, like ivy, were the growth of time" on the board. (Stevenson uses this phrase in his description of Mr. Utterson.) Ask students to identify the type of figure of speech this phrase exemplifies. ("His affections...were the growth of time" is a metaphor, and "like ivy" is a simile.) Talk about the literal meaning. Distribute the Figure of Speech worksheet and have students work in small groups to find examples in the novel. If you want the students to continue recording examples in the remaining chapters, assign a due date for the worksheet.

> Examples from the novel:
> *it was like some damned Juggernaut* (simile, metonymy)
> *about as emotional as a bagpipe* (simile)

HYPERBOLE	Extreme exaggeration used to describe a person or thing. Example: *She had as many pairs of shoes as there are stars in the sky.*
IRONY	The use of words to express something different from and often opposite to their literal meaning.
METAPHOR	A comparison without the words "like" or "as." Example: *The cat is a bag of bones.*
METONYMY	A figure of speech in which one word or phrase is substituted for another with which it is closely associated. Example: "Washington" for the United States government or "the sword" for military power.
ONOMATOPOEIA	The use of words such as "buzz" or "splash" that imitate the sounds associated with the objects or actions they refer to.
PARADOX	A seemingly self-contradictory statement that has some truth to it.
PERSONIFICATION	Attributing human characters to inanimate objects, animals, or ideas. Example: *the wind howled*
SIMILE	A comparison using the words "like" or "as."

FIGURES OF SPEECH *Dr. Jekyll and Mr. Hyde*

Figures of speech are literary devices that give the writer a non-literal way to describe images and events. The main types of figures of speech are hyperbole, irony, metaphor, metonymy, onomatopoeia, paradox, personification, and simile. Use the following chart to record examples of figures of speech used in *The Strange Case of Dr. Jekyll and Mr. Hyde*. A sample has been done for you. Note: In this novel you may not find an example of each *kind* of figure of speech.

FIGURE OF SPEECH	EXAMPLE & PAGE #	LITERAL MEANING
simile	about as emotional as a bagpipe	a bagpipe is an inanimate object and is not emotional

LESSON SIX

Objectives
1. To become familiar with the vocabulary for "Incident at the Window," "The Last Night," and "Dr. Lanyon's Narrative"
2. To preview the study questions for these chapters
3. To read these chapters
4. To identify examples of the four basic sentence structures

Activity 1
Give students about fifteen minutes to complete the prereading vocabulary worksheets and look at the study questions for "Incident at the Window," "The Last Night," and "Dr. Lanyon's Narrative."

Activity 2
Review the definitions of independent and subordinate clauses with students. (**Independent**: a clause that expresses a complete thought and can stand alone as a sentence. Example: "I shake hands on that, Richard." Subordinate (also called dependent): a clause that does not express a complete thought and cannot stand alone as a sentence. Example: "that was never lighted by a smile"

Activity 3
Introduce the four types of sentences with the following examples:
   Simple: one independent clause and no subordinate clauses
       Example: *"Yes, it is a bad story."*
   Compound: two or more independent clauses but no subordinate clauses
       Example: *"Hyde has gone to his account, and it only remains for us to find the body of your master."*
   Complex: one independent clause and at least one subordinate clause
       Example: *"If I am the chief of sinners, I am the chief of suffers also."*
   Compound-Complex: two or more independent clauses and at least one subordinate clause
       Example: *"Presently her eye wandered to the other, and she was surprised to recognize in him a certain Mr. Hyde, who had once visited her master and for whom she had conceived a dislike."*

Activity 4
The majority of the sentences in *The Strange Case of Dr. Jekyll and Mr. Hyde* are compound, complex, or compound-complex. You may want to divide your class into small groups and assign a type of sentence for each group to find examples of in the text. Another strategy is to copy several sentences onto the board or an overhead transparency and have students identify the types of sentences.

LESSON SEVEN

Objectives:
1. To discuss the main ideas and events in "Incident at the Window," "The Last Night," and "Dr. Lanyon's Narrative"
2. To identify character traits of Mr. Utterson and Dr. Jekyll

Activity 1
Have students work in small groups to discuss the answers to the study questions. Invite a representative from each group to present the group's answers to the class.

Activity 2 Mini-Lesson: Character Traits
Explain that an author creates characters by giving them traits such as physical attributes, thoughts, and feelings. The author develops these traits by telling what the characters say, do and think. Writers usually base their characters at least in part on a real person or persons, and then elaborate. A good writer will make the characters believable for the reader. A good writer will make the characters believable for the reader. it is up to the reader to get to know the characters by paying attention to stated traits and making inferences about others. Arrange the students in small groups and have them use the Character Traits Chart to being profiles of either Dr. Jekyll or Mr. Utterson. If you want students to continue with the Traits Chart, discuss it again during the Extra Discussion Questions in lesson 12 or in the Unit Review in Lesson 14.

LESSON EIGHT

Objectives
1. To understand plot development and record plot information on a chart
2. To become familiar with the vocabulary words for "Henry Jekyll's Full Statement of the Case"
3. To preview the study questions for that same chapter

Activity 1 Mini-Lesson: Plot
Tell students they will be discussing and mapping the plot of the novel. **Plot** refers to the events in the novel. It tells what the characters do, what happens to them, and how things happen. The plot is usually told in sequence. Plot structure is usually either conflict-resolution or goal-achievement. The main types of conflicts are character vs. character, character vs. nature, character vs. self, or character vs. society. In a goal-achievement plot structure, the main character sets a goal and the plot progresses until the goal is achieved or not achieved. The **climax** is the highest point of action or suspense. The reader does not yet know the outcome. The **resolution** or **outcome** occurs at the end of the story.

Use the Plot Diagram to help students identify the main conflicts and events in the novel so far. Tell them to complete the Plot Diagram after they read "Henry Jekyll's Full Statement of the Case." You may want to discuss plot again and check the diagrams during the Unit Review in Lesson 14.

CHARACTER TRAITS CHART *Dr. Jekyll and Mr. Hyde*

CHARACTER _____

Character Trait _____	Character Trait _____
Events That Show It:	Events That Show It:
Character Trait _____	Character Trait: _____
Events That Show It:	Events That Show It:

PLOT DIAGRAM *Dr. Jekyll and Mr. Hyde*

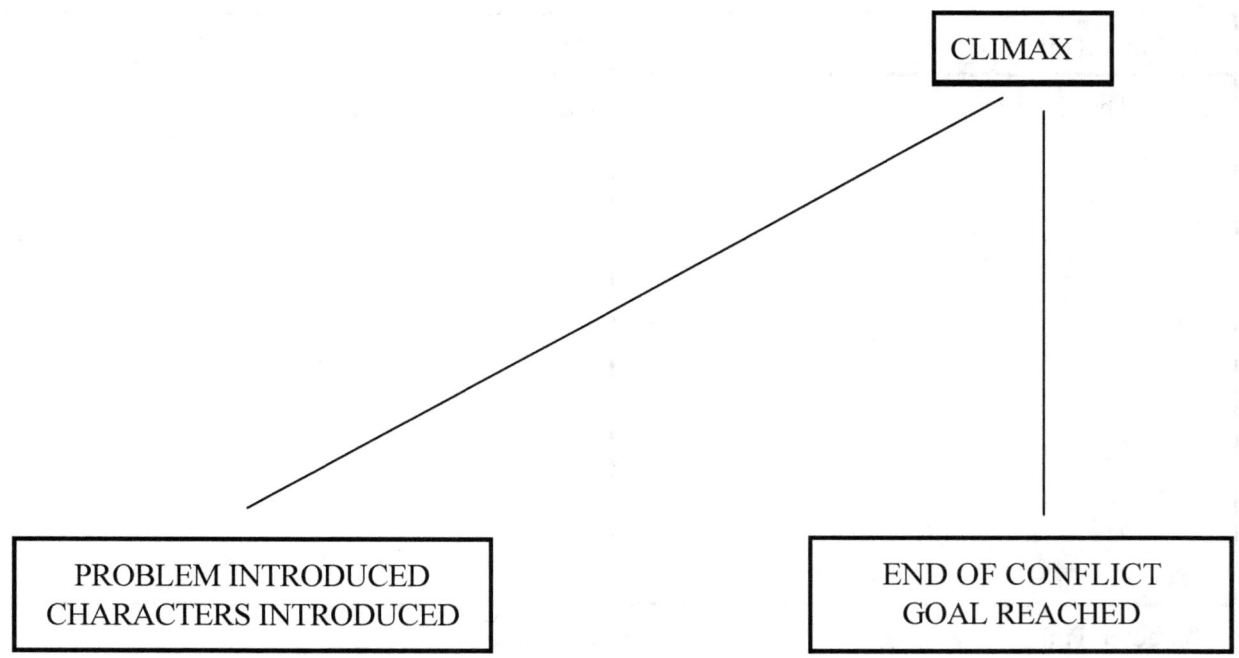

LESSON NINE

Objectives
> 1. To discuss and evaluate students' writing skills
> 2. To read "Henry Jekyll's Full Statement of the Case"
> 3. To work independently on study guide questions or writing assignments

Activity 1

Choose a quiet corner of the room and hold private writing conferences with individual students to discuss their work.

Activity 2

Have students work independently on reading "Henry Jekyll's Full Statement of the Case" and answer the study questions that go with that chapter.

Activity 3

If students complete Activity 2, they should use the remaining class time to complete their writing assignments, add information to the Plot Chart or Character Chart, or finish up other work related to this unit.

LESSON TEN

Objectives
> 1. To discuss the main ideas and events in "Henry Jekyll's Full Statement of the Case"
> 2. To complete a unit-related project

Activity 1

have students work in pairs or small groups to present skits that answer the study guide questions.

Activity 2

Allow students to choose one of the following projects. Give them the class period to complete it. If students need more time, you can assign the project as homework or add another day onto the unit.

1. Draw a book jacket that summarizes the story.
2. Write a critique of the book
3. Make a time line showing the important events from the story.
4. make a diorama or collage showing one of the scenes from the book.
5. Make puppets and write a puppet show to illustrate one scene from the story.
6. Write a radio or television commercial to advertise the book.
7. Design a poster to advertise the book.
8. Write a different ending to the story.
9. Make a two-sided mask showing Dr. Jekyll on one side and Mr. Hyde on the other.
10. Make a comic book version of the story to share with young readers.
11. make a mobile showing the main character, secondary characters, setting, and main events.
12. Create a poster describing a scene, a character, or one of the main themes.
13. Tape record a reading of a section of the book Include background music and sound effects.

LESSON ELEVEN

Objective
To have students practice writing to persuade

Activity 1
Ask students if they have ever seen a court trial. The defense attorney tries to persuade the jury and judge that his/her client is innocent. The prosecutor tries to persuade them the defendant is guilty. Tell them they will have the opportunity to either defend or prosecute Mr. Hyde for the murder of Sir Danvers Carew.

Activity 2
Distribute copies of Writing Assignment 3. Allow students to work on the assignment for the remainder of the class time. Set a due date for the assignment.

LESSON TWELVE

Objective
To discuss *The Strange Case of Dr. Jekyll and Mr. Hyde* at the interpretive and critical levels

Activity 1
Choose the questions from the Extra Writing Assignments/Discussion Questions which seem most appropriate for your students. A class discussion of these questions is most effective if students have been given the opportunity to formulate answers to the questions prior to the discussion. To this end, yo may either have all the students formulate answers to all the questions, divide the class into groups and assign one or more questions to each group, or you could assign one question to each student in your class. The option you choose will make a difference in the amount of class time needed for this activity.

Activity 2
After students have had ample time to formulate answers to the questions, begin your class discussion of the questions and the ideas presented by the questions. Be sure students take notes during the discussion so they have information to study for the test.

WRITING ASSIGNMENT 3 *Dr. Jekyll and Mr. Hyde*

PROMPT
Sir Danvers Carew, a Member of Parliament, was brutally murdered. A young woman said she saw Mr. Hyde do it. There were no other witnesses. In this writing assignment, Mr. Hyde is entitled to a trial by jury of London citizens. You are to act either as the defense (for Mr. Hyde) or the prosecution (against Mr. Hyde). Your assignment is to write a closing argument to the jury. (This is a lawyer's final summary of his/her case and the best efforts at persuading the jury to his/her side.)

PREWRITING
To begin, decide which side you want to take–the defense or the prosecution. On a piece of paper, jot down the main points, the facts which will support your case. Decide which points are your strongest and which of the arguments you will make are weaker. Organize your points from weakest to strongest and jot down anything you can think of which will support or explain your points.

DRAFTING
Begin with an introductory paragraph in which you introduce the jury to your side of the case. Follow that with one paragraph for each of the main points you have to support your case. Fill in each paragraph with examples and facts which support your main point. Then, write a paragraph in which you make your final closing statements.

PEER EDITING/REVISING
When you finish the rough draft of your paper, ask a student who sits near you to read it. After reading your rough draft, he/she should tell you what he/she liked best about your work, which parts were difficult to understand, and ways in which your work could be improved. Reread your paper considering your critic's comments, and make the corrections you think are necessary.

PROOFREADING
Do a final proofreading of your paper, double-checking your grammar, spelling, organization, and the clarity of your ideas.

EXTRA WRITING ASSIGNMENTS/DISCUSSION QUESTIONS
Dr. Jekyll and Mr. Hyde

Interpretive
1. From what point of view is the story written? How does this affect our understanding of the story?
2. What are the main conflicts in the story? Are they resolved? If so, how? If not, why not?
3. What is the setting? How important is the setting to the story? Why?
4. Is there a significance to the names Utterson, Jekyll, and Hyde? (Note: According to some critics, R. L. Stevenson originally intended the name Jekyll to have a French pronunciation, which would be *je kill*, with the accent on the second syllable. The pronoun *je* in French means *I*.)
5. Write a character sketch of Dr. Jekyll, Mr. Utterson, or Mr. Hyde.
6. Compare and contrast Dr. Jekyll's scientific theories with those of Dr. Lanyon.
7. Compare and contrast the physical and mental characteristics of Dr. Jekyll and Mr. Hyde.
8. Why do you think Mr. Utterson made so many incorrect assumptions?

Critical
9. Is this story believable? Why or why not?
10. How did Dr. Jekyll change over the course of the novel? Were these changes for the better?
11. Which characters were believable? Which, if any, were not?
12. The author often used vivid language to describe a scene or event. Give an example of his use of vivid language that you found most effective. Tell why it was effective.
12. What was the overall mood of the story? Give examples to support your answer.
13. How does the author create suspense?
14. What is the role or importance of the potion that Dr. Jekyll created?
15. What problem or conflict does the author use to get the story started? How effective is it?
16. Could any of the main events be left out? Which ones, if any? Why or why not?
17. Could you change the order of the main events and still have the same outcome? If not, how would the outcome change if the order of the events were changed?
18. How would the story have to change to have a different ending?
19. There are several narrators. How would the story change if there were just one narrator? Which character would you choose to be the single narrator? Why?
20. Which character do you know the most about? Which character do you know the least about?
21. Were you able to predict the ending? What clues did the author give?
22. Discuss the author's use of language. Is it natural? Do people you know talk the way the characters did?
23. Does the mood of the story change? How does the author show this?
24. What words does the author use to create the atmosphere of the book?
25. Which chapter was the most important? Why?
26. Were the descriptions in the book effective? Give some examples.
27. Which senses did the descriptions cause you to use? Give examples of the descriptions using hearing, seeing, touching, smelling, and taste.

Personal Response

28. Did you enjoy reading *The Strange Case of Dr. Jekyll and Mr. Hyde*?
29. Is *The Strange Case of Dr. Jekyll and Mr. Hyde* a good title for the book? Why or why not? If not, what title would you suggest?
30. What do you think Mr. Utterson will do next?
31. If you were Dr. Jekyll, what would you have done about Mr. Hyde?
32. Did you have strong feelings while reading this book? if so, what did the author do to cause those feelings? If not, why not?
33. Will you read more of Robert Louis Stevenson's books? Why or why not?
34. Did Henry Jekyll's experiences change the way you look at yourself? Explain how or why not.
35. Have you read any other stories similar to *The Strange Case of Dr. Jekyll and Mr. Hyde*? If so, tell about them.
36. Would you recommend this book to another student? Why or why not?
37. What makes Robert Louis Stevenson a unique and different writer?
38. What questions would you like to ask the author?
39. What was the saddest part of the story? What was the most exciting part?
40. What do you remember most about the story?
41. What did the book make you think about?

QUOTATIONS *Dr. Jekyll and Mr. Hyde*
Discuss the significance of the following quotations:

1. "Did you ever remark that door?" he asked; and when his companion had replied in the affirmative, "It is connected in my mind," he added, "with a very odd story."

2. "If you choose to make a capital out of this accident," said he, "I am naturally helpless. No gentleman but wishes to avoid a scene," says he. "Name your figure."

3. "He is not easy to describe. There is something wrong with his appearance; something displeasing, something down-right detestable. I never saw a man I so disliked, and yet I scarce know why. He must be deformed somewhere; he gives a strong feeling of deformity, although I couldn't specify the point. He's an extraordinary looking man, and yet I can name nothing out of the way. No, sir,; I can make no hand of it; I can't describe him. And it's not want of memory; for I declare I can see him this moment."

4. "I thought it was madness," he said, as he replaced the obnoxious paper in the safe, "and now I begin to fear it is disgrace."

5. "We had," was the reply. "But it is more than ten years since henry Jekyll became too fanciful for me. He began to go wrong, wrong in mind; and though of course I continue to take an interest in him for old time's sake, as they say, I see and I have seen devilish little of the man. Such unscientific balderdash," added the doctor, flushing suddenly purple, "would have estranged Damon and Pythias."

6. "If he be Mr. Hyde," he had thought, "I shall be Mr. Seek."

7. "Poor Harry Jekyll," he thought, "my mind misgives me he is in deep waters! He was wild when he was young; a long time ago to be sure; but in the law of God, there is no statute of limitations."

8. "I will tell you one thing: the moment I choose, I can be rid of Mr. Hyde. I give you my hand upon that; and I thank you again and again; and I will add just one little word, Utterson, that I am sure you'll take in good part: this is a private matter, and I beg of you to let it sleep."

9. "I have really a very great interest in poor Hyde. I know you have seen him; he told me so; and I fear he was rude. But I do sincerely take a great, a very great interest in that young man; and if I am taken away, Utterson, I wish you to promise me that you will bear with me and get his rights for him. I think you would, if you knew all; and it would be a weight off my mind if you would promise."

10. "Ah!" said she, "he is in trouble! What has he done?"

11. "Utterson, I swear to God," cried the doctor, "I swear to God I will never set eyes on him again. I bind my honour to you that I am done with him in this world. It is all at an end. And indeed he does not want my help; you do no t know him as I do; he is safe, he is quite safe, mark my words, he will never more be heard of."

12. "I have had a lesson–O God, Utterson, what a lesson I have had!"

13. "Well, sir," returned the clerk, "there's a rather singular resemblance; the two hands are in many points identical: only differently sloped."

14. "I have had a shock," he said, "and I shall never recover. It is a question of weeks. Well, life has been pleasant; I liked it; yes, sir, I used to like it. I sometimes think if we knew all, we should be more glad to get away."

15. "You must suffer me to go my own dark way. I have brought on myself a punishment and a danger that I cannot name. If I am the chief of sinners, I am the chief of sufferers also."

16. "I think there's been foul play."

17. "For God's sake," he added, "find me some of the old."

18. "We have come too late," he said sternly, "whether to save or to punish. Hyde is gone to his account; and it only remains for us to find the body of your master."

19. "Have you got it?" he cried. "Have you got it?"

20. "What he told me in the next our, I cannot bring my mind to set on paper. I saw what I saw, I heard what I heard, and my soul sickened at it; and yet now when that sight has faded from my eyes, I ask myself if I believe it, and I cannot answer. My life is shaken to its roots; sleep has left me; the deadliest terror sits by me at all hours of the day and night, and I feel that my days are numbered, and that I must die; and yet I shall die incredulous."

21. ". . . I thus drew steadily nearer to that truth, by whose partial discovery I have been doomed to such a dreadful shipwreck: that man is not truly one, but truly two."

22. "My devil had long be caged, he came out roaring."

23. "Here then, as I lay down the pen and proceed to seal up my confession, I bring the life of that unhappy Henry Jekyll to an end."

LESSON THIRTEEN

Objective
> To review all of the vocabulary work done in this unit

Activity

Choose one (or more) of the vocabulary review activities listed on the next page and spend your class period as directed in the activity. Some of the materials for these review activities are located in the Vocabulary Resources section in this unit.

VOCABULARY REVIEW ACTIVITIES

1. Divide your class into two teams and have an old-fashioned spelling or definition bee.
2. Give each of your students (or students in groups of two, three or four) a *Jekyll and Hyde* Vocabulary Word Search Puzzle. The person (group) to find all of the vocabulary words in the puzzle first wins.
3. Give students a *Jekyll and Hyde* Vocabulary Word Search Puzzle without the word list. The person or group to find the most vocabulary words in the puzzle wins.
4. Use a *Jekyll and Hyde* Vocabulary Crossword Puzzle. Put the puzzle onto a transparency on the overhead projector (so everyone can see it), and do the puzzle together as a class.
5. Give students a *Jekyll and Hyde* Vocabulary Matching Work sheet to do.
6. Divide your class into two teams. Use the *Jekyll and Hyde* vocabulary words with their letters jumbled as a word list. Student 1 from Team A faces off against Student 1 from Team B. You write the first jumbled word on the board. The first student (1A or 1B) to unscramble the word wins the chance for his/her team to score points. If 1A wins the jumble, go to student 2A and give him/her a definition. He/she must give you the correct spelling of the vocabulary word which fits that definition. If he/she does, Team A scores a point, and you give student 3A a definition for which you expect a correctly spelled matching vocabulary word. Continue giving Team A definitions until some team member makes an incorrect response. An incorrect response sends the game back to the jumbled-word face off, this time with students 2A and 2B. Instead of repeating giving definitions to the first few students of each team, continue with the student after the one who gave the last incorrect response on the team. For example, if Team B wins the jumbled-word face-off, and student 5B gave the last incorrect answer for Team B, you would start this round of definition questions with student 6B, and so on. The team with the most points wins!
7. Have students write a story in which they correctly use as many vocabulary words as possible. Have students read their compositions orally. Post the most original compositions on your bulletin board.

LESSON FOURTEEN

Objective
>   To review the main ideas presented in *Dr. Jekyll and Mr. Hyde*

Activity #1
  Choose one of the review games/activities included in this unit and spend your class period as outlined there. Some materials for these activities are located in the Unit Resources section of this unit.

Activity #2
Remind students that the Unit Test will be in the next class meeting. Stress the review of the Study Guides and their class notes as a last minute, brush-up review for the unit test.

REVIEW GAMES/ACTIVITIES - *Dr. Jekyll and Mr. Hyde*

1. Ask the class to make up a unit test for *Dr. Jekyll and Mr. Hyde*. The test should have 4 sections: matching, true/false, short answer, and essay. Students may use 1/2 period to make the test and then swap papers and use the other 1/2 class period to take a test a classmate has devised (open book). You may want to use the unit test included in this unit or take questions from the students' unit tests to formulate your own test.

2. Take 1/2 period for students to make up true and false questions (including the answers). Collect the papers and divide the class into two teams. Draw a big tic-tac-toe board on the chalk board. Make one team X and one team O. Ask questions to each side, giving each student one turn. If the question is answered correctly, that students' team's letter (X or O) is placed in the box. If the answer is incorrect, no mark is placed in the box. The object is to get three marks in a row like tic-tac-toe. You may want to keep track of the number of games won for each team.

3. Take 1/2 period for students to make up questions (true/false and short answer). Collect the questions. Divide the class into two teams. You'll alternate asking questions to individual members of teams A & B (like in a spelling bee). The question keeps going from A to B until it is correctly answered, then a new question is asked. A correct answer does not allow the team to get another question. Correct answers are +2 points; incorrect answers are -1 point.

4. Have students pair up and quiz each other from their study guides and class notes.

5. Give students a *Dr. Jekyll and Mr. Hyde* crossword puzzle to complete.

6. Divide your class into two teams. Use the *Dr. jekyll and Mr. Hyde* crossword words with their letters jumbled as a word list. Student 1 from Team A faces off against Student 1 from Team B. You write the first jumbled word on the board. The first student (1A or 1B) to unscramble the word wins the chance for his/her team to score points. If 1A wins the jumble, go to student 2A and give him/her a clue. He/she must give you the correct word which matches that clue. If he/she does, Team A scores a point, and you give student 3A a clue for which you expect another correct response. Continue giving Team A clues until some team member makes an incorrect response. An incorrect response sends the game back to the jumbled-word face off, this time with students 2A and 2B. Instead of repeating giving clues to the first few students of each team, continue with the student after the one who gave the last incorrect response on the team. For example, if Team B wins the jumbled-word face-off, and student 5B gave the last incorrect answer for Team B, you would start this round of clue questions with student 6B, and so on.

UNIT TESTS

SHORT ANSWER UNIT TEST 1 *The Strange Case of Dr. Jekyll and Mr. Hyde*

I. Matching/ Identify

____ 1. Dr. Jekyll
____ 2. Mr. Hyde
____ 3. Mr. Utterson
____ 4. Mr. Enfield
____ 5. Dr. Lanyon
____ 6. Sir Danvers Carew
____ 7. Poole
____ 8. Bradshaw
____ 9. evil
____ 10. composite

A. murderer
B. Mr. Hyde's personality
C. witnessed the girl's trampling
D. suspected foul play
E. studied the dual nature of man
F. murder victim
G. had the doctor's will
H. Dr. Jekyll's personality
I. died after he learned the secret
J. footman who helped break down the door

II. Short Answer

1. Summarize Mr. Enfield's story. Include the way Mr. Enfield said he felt about the man.

2. Describe the murder. Tell when it happened in relation to the rest of the story. Give the name of the murderer, the victim, and tell who saw the murder. Describe what the murdered man was carrying. Tell who identified the body.

Short Answer Unit Test 1 *The Strange Case of Dr. Jekyll and Mr. Hyde*

3. Where did Mr. Utterson and Mr. Enfield go for their Sunday walk? Whom did they see? What happened? How did they react?

4. Whom and what did Poole, Bradshaw, and Mr. Utterson find when they broke the door down?

5. Discuss the importance of the following quotation: "I have had a shock," he said, "and I shall never recover. It is a question of weeks. Well, life has been pleasant; I liked it; yes, sir, I used to like it. I sometimes think if we knew all, we should be more glad to get away."

Short Answer Unit Test 1 *The Strange Case of Dr. Jekyll and Mr. Hyde*

III. Fill-in-the-Blank

1. Dr. Henry Jekyll thought one of his worst faults was his _____, because he wanted to appear serious to the general public.

2. He directed his studies towards man's _____.

3. He thought if each could be housed in _____, life would be more bearable.

4. Dr. Jekyll compounded a _____ that would accomplish what he was trying to do.

5. When Mr. Hyde appeared, Dr. Jekyll noticed that he (Hyde) was somewhat _____

6. Dr. Jekyll believed that _____ had deformed Mr. Hyde.

7. After a while, Dr. Jekyll began to _____ without warning.

8. The _____ of being Mr. Hyde terrified Dr. Jekyll.

9. Mr. Hyde _____ the necessity of returning to Dr. Jekyll's form.

10. Dr. Jekyll's original chemical provisions were running low, and his new supply was not effective. He concluded that an _____ in the first supply caused the changes. Dr. Jekyll managed to make enough of the formula from his first supply to take a final draught and die.

Short Answer Unit Test 1 *The Strange Case of Dr. Jekyll and Mr. Hyde*

V. Vocabulary Part 1

Listen to the vocabulary words and spell them. After you have spelled all the words, go back and write down the definitions.

WORD	DEFINITION
1.	
2.	
3.	
4.	
5.	
6.	
7.	
8.	
9.	
10.	

Vocabulary Part 2

____ 1. eminently   A. grieving; expressing sorrow
____ 2. reprove   B. hateful; nasty
____ 3. detestable   C. relating to money
____ 4. iniquity   D. unable to express one's thoughts clearly
____ 5. incoherency   E. rebuke; scold
____ 6. conflagration   F. puzzles
____ 7. lamentation   G. wickedness
____ 8. enigmas   H. varied; greatly diversified
____ 9. multifarious   I. a great fire
____ 10. pecuniary   J. outstanding

Answer Key Short Answer Unit Test 1 *The Strange Case of Dr. Jekyll and Mr. Hyde*

I. Matching/Identify

E	1.	Dr. Jekyll	A.	murderer
A	2.	Mr. Hyde	B.	Mr. Hyde's personality
G	3.	Mr. Utterson	C.	witnessed the girl's trampling
C	4.	Mr. Enfield	D.	suspected foul play
I	5.	Dr. Lanyon	E.	studied the dual nature of man
F	6.	Sir Danvers Carew	F.	murder victim
D	7.	Poole	G.	had the doctor's will
J	8.	Bradshaw	H.	Dr. Jekyll's personality
B	9.	evil	I.	died after he learned the secret
H	10.	composite	J.	footman who helped break down the door

II. Short Answer

1. Summarize Mr. Enfield's story. Include the way Mr. Enfield said he felt about the man. Give the man's name.

    Mr. Enfield was on his way home at about 3 AM on a black winter morning. He saw a little man walking eastward, and girl of about 8 or 10 running down a cross street. They ran into each other. The man trampled over the girl and left her screaming on the ground. Mr. Enfield ran after the man and brought him back to the girl. By then the girl's family and the doctor were there. The girl was frightened, but not badly hurt. The man offered money to the girl's family, and they asked for 100 pounds. He used a key to go in through the door. He came back with a check for 90 pounds and 10 pounds in gold coins. The check was signed by a well-known person. Mr. Enfield had taken a loathing to the man at first sight. The man was Mr. Hyde.

2. Describe the murder. Tell when it happened in relation to the rest of the story. Give the name of the murderer, the victim, and tell who saw the murder. Describe what the murdered man was carrying. Tell who identified the body.

    The murder took place about a year after the previous chapter. Sir Danvers Carew, a Member of Parliament, was murdered near midnight. A maid was looking out her window and saw the entire murder. She recognized Mr. Hyde, who hit the victim with a cane and then trampled him. Sir Carew was carrying a purse, a gold watch, and a sealed envelope addressed to Mr. Utterson. Mr. Utterson identified the body.

3. Where did Mr. Utterson and Mr. Enfield go for their Sunday walk? Whom did they see? What happened? How did they react?

They went past Mr. Hyde's door, and decided to go into the courtyard and try to see Dr. Jekyll. He was sitting in the window and they conversed for a few minutes. He said he could not come down, and did not want to invite them up, but agreed with Mr. Utterson to chat from where they were. Suddenly his face got "an expression of abject terror and despair." The two men left the courtyard. They were pale and had a look of horror in their eyes.

4. Whom and what did Poole, Bradshaw, and Mr. Utterson find when they broke the door down?
They found Edward Hyde, dressed in clothes that were too big for him. However, the clothes would have fit the doctor. Mr. Hyde was dead. They also found piles of the white salt and other traces of chemical works. Mr. Utterson found an envelope in the doctor's handwriting that was addressed to him (Utterson.)

5. Discuss the importance of the following quotation: "I have had a shock," he said, "and I shall never recover. It is a question of weeks. Well, life has been pleasant; I liked it; yes, sir, I used to like it. I sometimes think if we knew all, we should be more glad to get away."
Mr. Utterson was visiting Dr. Lanyon. He remarked that Dr. Lanyon did not look well. This was part of Dr. Lanyon's reply.

III. Fill-in-the-Blank
1. Dr. Henry Jekyll thought one of his worst faults was his **gaiety**, because he wanted to appear serious to the general public.
2. He directed his studies towards man's **dual nature**.
3. He thought if each could be housed in **separate identities**, life would be more bearable.
4. Dr. Jekyll compounded a **drug** that would accomplish what he was trying to do.
5. When Mr. Hyde appeared, Dr. Jekyll noticed that he was somewhat **smaller** slighter, and younger than Henry Jekyll.
6. Dr. Jekyll believed that **evil** had deformed Mr. Hyde.
7. After a while, Dr. Jekyll began to **transform** without warning.
8. The **horror** of being Mr. Hyde terrified Dr. Jekyll.
9. Mr. Hyde **hated** the necessity of returning to Dr. Jekyll's form.
10. Dr. Jekyll's original chemical provisions were running low, and his new supply was not effective. He concluded that an **impurity** in the first supply caused the changes. Dr. Jekyll managed to make enough of the formula from his first supply to take a final draught and die.

IV. Essay
What are the main conflicts in the story? Are they resolved? If so, how? If not, why not?
Answers will vary, according to the nature of the previous classroom discussions.

Answer Key Short Answer Unit Test 1 *The Strange Case of Dr. Jekyll and Mr. Hyde*

V. Vocabulary Part 1

WORD	DEFINITION
1.	
2.	
3.	
4.	
5.	
6.	
7.	
8.	
9.	
10.	

Vocabulary Part 2

J	1.	eminently	A.	grieving; expressing sorrow
E	2.	reprove	B.	hateful; nasty
B	3.	detestable	C.	relating to money
G	4.	iniquity	D.	unable to express one's thoughts clearly
D	5.	incoherency	E.	rebuke; scold
I	6.	conflagration	F.	puzzles
A	7.	lamentation	G.	wickedness
F	8.	enigmas	H.	varied; greatly diversified
H	9.	multifarious	I.	a great fire
C	10.	pecuniary	J.	outstanding

SHORT ANSWER UNIT TEST 2 *The Strange Case of Dr. Jekyll and Mr. Hyde*

I. Matching/ Identify

_____ 1. cane
_____ 2. cheque book
_____ 3. red
_____ 4. purple
_____ 5. green
_____ 6. drawer
_____ 7. midnight
_____ 8. six
_____ 9. three
_____ 10. ten

A. first color of the liquid
B. third color of the liquid
C. time the messenger came
D. AM time when girl was trampled
E. half of one was behind the door
F. # of years since Dr. Lanyon had seen Dr. Jekyll
G. # of hours Dr. Jekyll could keep from changing
H. Dr. Lanyon held it for Dr. Jekyll
I. second color of the liquid
J. part of one was in the fire

II. Short Answer

1. Poole said Dr. Jekyll had been asking for something all week. How was he asking for it? What was it? What type did he want?

2. Describe all of the changes in Dr. Jekyll after Mr. Hyde's disappearance. What did he say about seeing Dr. Lanyon again?

Short Answer Unit Test 2 *The Strange Case of Dr. Jekyll and Mr. Hyde*

3. Summarize the discussion between Dr. Jekyll and Mr. Utterson after the dinner party.

4. What conclusion did Dr. Jekyll draw about the original powder?

5. Describe, in order, the process Dr. Jekyll went through when he prepared his tincture. Include the results.

Short Answer Unit Test 2 *The Strange Case of Dr. Jekyll and Mr. Hyde*

III. Fill-in-the-Blank

1. Mr. Utterson had charge of Dr. Jekyll's _____.

2. _____ was the first person in the story to talk about seeing Mr. Hyde.
3. Mr. Utterson went to see _____ to discuss his concerns about Dr. Jekyll.
4. Poole told Mr. Utterson that Mr. Hyde came and went by means of the _____.
5. Dr. Lanyon _____ about three weeks after the visit by Dr. Jekyll.
6. The envelope from Dr. Lanyon said if Mr. Utterson died before he got it, the enclosed letter should be _____.
7. Poole suspected that Dr. Jekyll was the victim of some kind of _____.
8. Henry Jekyll studied the _____ of man.
9. Dr. Jekyll said Mr. Hyde _____ him.
10. Dr. Jekyll concluded that the first batch of chemical salt had some _____ that caused the changes.

IV. Essay

Compare and contrast the physical and mental characteristics of Dr. Jekyll and Mr. Hyde.

Short Answer Unit Test 2 *The Strange Case of Dr. Jekyll and Mr. Hyde*

V. Vocabulary Part 1

Listen to the vocabulary words and spell them. After you have spelled all the words, go back and write down the definitions.

WORD	DEFINITION
1.	
2.	
3.	
4.	
5.	
6.	
7.	
8.	
9.	
10.	

Vocabulary Part 2

Directions: Place the letter of the matching definition on the blank line.

___	1. capacious		A.	firm dislikes
___	2. aversions		B.	beginning; in an early stage
___	3. incongruous		C.	diligently
___	4. inveterately		D.	provided
___	5. endowed		E.	absurd; incompatible
___	6. incipient		F.	excessive
___	7. exorbitant		G.	deep rooted; habitually
___	8. disconsolate		H.	large
___	9. sedulously		I.	pondered; reflected over and over
___	10. ruminated		J.	sad

Answer Key Short Answer Unit Test 2 *The Strange Case of Dr. Jekyll and Mr. Hyde*

I. Matching/ Identify

E	1.	cane	A.	first color of the liquid
J	2.	cheque book	B.	third color of the liquid
A	3.	red	C.	time the messenger came
I	4.	purple	D.	AM time when girl was trampled
B	5.	green	E.	half of one was behind the door
H	6.	drawer	F.	# of years since Dr. Lanyon had seen Dr. Jekyll
C	7.	midnight	G.	# of hours Dr. Jekyll could keep from changing
G	8.	six	H.	Dr. Lanyon held it for Dr. Jekyll
D	9.	three	I.	second color of the liquid
F	10.	ten	J.	part of one was in the fire

II. Short Answer

1. Poole said Dr. Jekyll had been asking for something all week. How was he asking for it? What was it? What type did he want?
    He had been writing notes and throwing them on the steps. The notes instructed Poole to go to the wholesale chemists in town to buy a certain type of drug. The last letter asked the Messrs. Maw to "find him some of the old."

2. Describe all of the changes in Dr. Jekyll after Mr. Hyde's disappearance. What did he say about seeing Dr. Lanyon again?
    For about two months it seemed that Dr. Jekyll was back to his old self. He entertained, and he looked much better. Then, suddenly, he stopped seeing people. In response to Mr. Utterson's letter about Dr. Lanyon, Dr. Jekyll agreed that the two must never meet again. Dr. Jekyll said he was going to lead a life of seclusion.

3. Summarize the discussion between Dr. Jekyll and Mr. Utterson after the dinner party.
    Mr. Utterson told Dr. Jekyll he was concerned about the provisions of the will. He disapproved because of some new information he had about Mr. Hyde. Dr. Jekyll told Mr. Utterson things were not that bad, and he could be rid of Mr. Hyde if he wanted to. He asked Utterson to help Hyde if and when Dr. Jekyll was no longer around. Mr. Utterson reluctantly agreed.

4. What conclusion did Dr. Jekyll draw about the original powder?
    It had an impurity that made the potion effective.

5. Describe, in order, the process Dr. Jekyll went through when he prepared his tincture. Include the results.

> He bought the salt from a chemical wholesale company. He compounded the elements and drank the potion. He experienced racking pangs, grinding bones, nausea, and a horror of the spirit. Then he came to himself and felt younger and livelier. He knew he was more wicked. He was aware he was shorter. He became Mr. Hyde.

III. Fill-in-the-Blank
1. Mr. Utterson had charge of Dr. Jekyll's **will**.
2. **Mr. Enfield** was the first person in the story to talk about seeing Mr. Hyde.
3. Mr. Utterson went to see **Dr. Lanyon** to discuss his concerns about Dr. Jekyll.
4. Poole told Mr. Utterson that Mr. Hyde came and went by means of the **laboratory**.
5. Dr. Lanyon **died about** three weeks after the visit by Dr. Jekyll.
6. The envelope from Dr. Lanyon said if Mr. Utterson died before he got it, the enclosed letter should be **destroyed unread**.
7. Poole suspected that Dr. Jekyll was the victim of some kind of **foul play**.
8. Henry Jekyll studied the **dual nature** of man.
9. Dr. Jekyll said Mr. Hyde **hated/despised** him.
10. Dr. Jekyll concluded that the first batch of chemical salt had some **impurities** that caused the changes.

IV. Essay
Compare and contrast the physical and mental characteristics of Dr. Jekyll and Mr. Hyde.

Answers will vary depending on the extent of previous classroom discussion.

V. Vocabulary Part 1

	WORD	DEFINITION
1.		
2.		
3.		
4.		
5.		
6.		
7.		
8.		
9.		
10.		

Answer Key Short Answer Unit Test 2 *The Strange Case of Dr. Jekyll and Mr. Hyde*

Vocabulary Part 2 Note: Also use this key for the Advanced Short Answer Unit Test.
Directions: Place the letter of the matching definition on the blank line.

H	1.	capacious	A.	firm dislikes
A	2.	aversions	B.	beginning; in an early stage
E	3.	incongruous	C.	diligently
G	4.	inveterately	D.	provided
D	5.	endowed	E.	absurd; incompatible
B	6.	incipient	F.	excessive
F	7.	exorbitant	G.	deep rooted; habitually
J	8.	disconsolate	H.	large
C	9.	sedulously	I.	pondered; reflected over and over
I	10.	ruminated	J.	sad

ADVANCED SHORT ANSWER UNIT TEST *The Strange Case of Dr. Jekyll and Mr. Hyde*

I. Matching/ Identify

____ 1. cane
____ 2. cheque book
____ 3. red
____ 4. purple
____ 5. green
____ 6. drawer
____ 7. midnight
____ 8. six
____ 9. three
____ 10. ten

A. first color of the liquid
B. third color of the liquid
C. time the messenger came
D. AM time when girl was trampled
E. half of one was behind the door
F. # of years since Dr. Lanyon had seen Dr. Jekyll
G. # of hours Dr. Jekyll could keep from changing
H. Dr. Lanyon held it for Dr. Jekyll
I. second color of the liquid
J. part of one was in the fire

II. Short Answer

1. Write a character sketch of Dr. Jekyll, Mr. Hyde, or Mr. Utterson.

2. How did Dr. Jekyll change over the course of the novel? Which changes were for the better? Which were not?

Advanced Short Answer Unit Test *The Strange Case of Dr. Jekyll and Mr. Hyde*

3. Why do you think Mr. Utterson made so many incorrect assumptions?

4. How did Robert Louis Stevenson create suspense? Use examples from the novel to support your answer.

5. Did you have strong feelings while reading this book? If so, what did the author do to cause those feelings? If not, why not?

Advanced Short Answer Unit Test *The Strange Case of Dr. Jekyll and Mr. Hyde*

III. <u>Quotations</u>
Discuss the significance of the following quotations.
1. "Did you ever remark that door?" he asked; and when his companion had replied in the affirmative, "It is connected in my mind," he added, "with a very odd story."

2. "If he be Mr. Hyde," he had thought, "I shall be Mr. Seek."

3. "Utterson, I swear to God, I swear to God I will never set eyes on him again. I bind my honour to you that I am done with him in this world. It is all at an end. And indeed he does not want my help; you do not know him as I do; he is safe, he is quite safe, mark my words, he will never more be heard of."

4. "What he told me in the next hour, I cannot bring my mind to set on paper. I saw what I saw, I heard what I herd, and my soul sickened at it; and yet now when that sight has faded from my eyes, I ask myself if I believe, it, and I cannot answer. My life is shaken to its roots; sleep has left me; the deadliest terror sits by me at all hours of the day and night, and I feel that my days are numbered, and that I must die; and yet I shall die incredulous."

5. "For God's sake," he added, "find me some of the old."

Advanced Short Answer Unit Test *The Strange Case of Dr. Jekyll and Mr. Hyde*

IV. Vocabulary

Listen to the words and write them down. After you have written down all of the words, write a paragraph in which you use all of the words. The paragraph must in some way relate to *The Strange Case of Dr. Jekyll and Mr. Hyde*.

1. _____
2. _____
3. _____
4. _____
5. _____

6. _____
7. _____
8. _____
9. _____
10. _____

MULTIPLE CHOICE UNIT TEST 1 *The Strange Case of Dr. Jekyll and Mr. Hyde*

I. Matching/ Identify

1. Dr. Jekyll
2. Mr. Hyde
3. Mr. Utterson
4. Mr. Enfield
5. Dr. Lanyon
6. Sir Danvers Carew
7. Poole
8. Bradshaw
9. evil
10. composite

A. murderer
B. Mr. Hyde's personality
C. witnessed the girl's trampling
D. suspected foul play
E. studied the dual nature of man
F. murder victim
G. had the doctor's will
H. Dr. Jekyll's personality
I. died after he learned the secret
J. footman who helped break down the door

II. Multiple Choice

1. Who is being described? He was cold and never smiled. He was tall and lean. He tolerated others, and was more inclined to help than to reprove.
   A. Mr. Utterson
   B. Dr. Jekyll
   C. Mr. Richard Enfield
   D. Poole

2. Which of the following statements was **not** included in Mr. Enfield's story?
   A. Mr. Enfield ran after the man and brought him back.
   B. The family beat the man.
   C. The man gave the family a check signed by a well-known person.
   D. A little man trampled over a young girl and left her screaming on the ground.

3. Which phrase in Dr. Jekyll's will bothered his lawyer?
   A. Mr. Hyde was Dr. Jekyll's nephew and should receive a monthly allowance.
   B. Dr. Jekyll wanted to leave all of his possessions to Mr. Hyde.
   C. The lawyer was to do whatever Mr. Hyde wanted.
   D. If Dr. Jekyll disappeared for more than three months, Mr. Hyde should step into his shoes.

4. True or False: Dr. Lanyon disagreed with some of Dr. Jekyll's scientific ideas.
   A. True
   B. False

Multiple Choice Unit Test 1 *The Strange Case of Dr. Jekyll and Mr. Hyde*

5. Which of the statements about the murder is **false?**
   A. A maid was looking out her window and saw the entire murder.
   B. Sir Danvers Carew, a Member of Parliament, was murdered near midnight.
   C. The murdered man was carrying an envelope addressed to Dr. Jekyll.
   D. The murder took place about a year after the previous chapter.

6. What did Mr. Guest discover?
   A. The fingerprints on the note belonged to Dr. Jekyll.
   B. Mr. Hyde's writing strongly resembled Dr. Jekyll's writing.
   C. The note paper had traces of a poison on it.
   D. The ink was still wet, which meant the note had been written about an hour earlier.

7. True or False: While conversing with Dr. Jekyll, Mr. Utterson and Mr. Enfield watched the doctor's face get an expression of terror and despair.
   A. True
   B. False

8. What had Dr. Jekyll had been asking for all week?
   A. He had been asking for Mr. Utterson to visit him.
   B. He had been asking for paper to write to Mr. Hyde.
   C. He had been asking for a lot of food to be brought to his laboratory.
   D. He had been asking for some of the old drug.

9. Who had received a note from Dr. Jekyll giving instructions?
   A. the housekeeper
   B. Poole
   C. Dr. Lanyon
   D. Inspector Newcomen

10. True or False: Dr. Jekyll found it bothersome to feel so light-hearted, because he wanted to appear serious to the public.
    A. True
    B. False

Multiple Choice Unit Test 1 *The Strange Case of Dr. Jekyll and Mr. Hyde*

III. Quotations

Directions: Write the letter for the speaker on the answer sheet.

A. Dr. Jekyll	B. Mr. Hyde	C. Mr. Utterson	D. Poole
E. Dr. Lanyon	F. Mr. Enfield	G. Mr. Guest	H. Housekeeper

1. "Did you ever remark that door? It is connected in my mind with a very odd story."

2. "If you choose to make a capital out of this accident, I am naturally helpless. No gentleman but wishes to avoid a scene. Name your figure."

3. "If he be Mr. Hyde, I shall be Mr. Seek."

4. "I thought it was madness, and now I begin to fear it is disgrace."

5. "He began to go wrong, wrong in mind; and though of course I continue to take an interest in him for old time's sake, as they say, I see and I have seen devilish little of the man. Such unscientific balderdash would have estranged Damon and Pythias."

6. "Ah! He is in trouble! What has he done?"

7. "Well sir, there's a rather singular resemblance; the two hands are in many points identical: only differently sloped."

8. "I have had a shock," and I shall never recover. It is a question of weeks. Well, life has been pleasant; I liked it; yes, sir, I used to like it. I sometimes think if we knew all, we should be more glad to get away."

9. "I think there's been foul play."

10. "My devil had long be caged, he came out roaring."

Multiple Choice Unit Test 1 *The Strange Case of Dr. Jekyll and Mr. Hyde*

IV. Vocabulary Part 1

1. eminently
2. reprove
3. detestable
4. iniquity
5. incoherency
6. conflagration
7. lamentation
8. enigmas
9. multifarious
10. pecuniary

A. grieving; expressing sorrow
B. hateful; nasty
C. relating to money
D. unable to express one's thoughts clearly
E. rebuke; scold
F. puzzles
G. wickedness
H. varied; greatly diversified
I. a great fire
J. outstanding

Vocabulary Part 2   Directions: Circle the letter next to the word that matches the definition.

11. **strict; stern**
    a. reprove
    b. capacious
    c. austere
    d. odious

12. **a person under the support of a patron**
    a. calamity
    b. protégé
    c. gaunt
    d. insensate

13. **reflected over and over**
    a. iniquity
    b. conflagration
    c. ruminated
    d. pecuniary

14. **without feeling**
    a. austere
    b. incongruous
    c. volatile
    d. insensate

15. **lean and angular**
    a. endowed
    b. gaunt
    c. multifarious
    d. incipient

16. **gloomy; depressing**
    a. pecuniary
    b. exorbitant
    c. abject
    d. sombre

17. **to place trust in**
    a. reprove
    b. accosted
    c. scrutiny
    d. repose

18. **excessive**
    a. austere
    b. insensate
    c. exorbitant
    d. sombre

19. **hateful**
    a. odious
    b. abject
    c. insensate
    d. mien

20. **diligently**
    a. capacious
    b. perplexity
    c. sedulously
    d. eminently

MULTIPLE CHOICE UNIT TEST 2 *The Strange Case of Dr. Jekyll and Mr. Hyde*

I. Matching/ Identify

1. cane
2. cheque book
3. red
4. purple
5. green
6. drawer
7. midnight
8. six
9. three
10. ten

A. first color of the liquid
B. third color of the liquid
C. time the messenger came
D. AM time when girl was trampled
E. half of one was behind the door
F. # of years since Dr. Lanyon had seen Dr. Jekyll
G. # of hours Dr. Jekyll could keep from changing
H. Dr. Lanyon held it for Dr. Jekyll
I. second color of the liquid
J. part of one was in the fire

II. Multiple Choice

1. What did Mr. Utterson and Mr. Enfield see that reminded Mr. Enfield of an odd story?
    A. They saw a broken second story window.
    B. They saw a rotting tree trunk.
    C. They saw a blistered and distainted door.
    D. They saw a bent street sign.

2. True or False: Mr. Enfield had charge of Dr. Jekyll's will.
    A. True
    B. False

3. Which of these was **not** one of the feelings Mr. Utterson expressed for Mr. Hyde?
    A. pity
    B. disgust
    C. fear
    D. loathing

4. What did Mr. Utterson agree to do for Dr. Jekyll?
    A. He agreed to hold onto the will for one year.
    B. He agreed to find a house for Mr. Hyde.
    C. He agreed to invite Dr. Lanyon and Dr. Jekyll to a dinner together.
    D. He agreed to help Mr. Hyde if the doctor were no longer around.

5. Which of the statements about the murder is **false?**
    A. A maid was looking out her window and saw the entire murder.
    B. Sir Danvers Carew, a Member of Parliament, was murdered near midnight.
    C. The murdered man was carrying an envelope addressed to Dr. Jekyll.
    D. The murder took place about a year after the previous chapter.

Multiple Choice Unit Test 2 *The Strange Case of Dr. Jekyll and Mr. Hyde*

6. What did Mr. Utterson and Inspector Newcomen find at Mr. Hyde's house?
    A. They found Dr. Jekyll's scientific log book.
    B. They found the murdered man's gold watch and chain.
    C. They found Mr. Hyde, asleep.
    D. They found the other half of the cane that was used in the murder.

7. What happened to Dr. Lanyon?
    A. He left the country and was never heard from again.
    B. He renewed his friendship with Dr. Jekyll.
    C. He died a few weeks after Mr. Utterson's visit.
    D. He went insane and was committed to an asylum.

8. True or False: While conversing with Dr. Jekyll, Mr. Utterson and Mr. Enfield watched the doctor's face get an expression of terror and despair.
    A. True
    B. False

9. Which was **not** found when Poole, Bradshaw, and Mr. Utterson broke the door down?
    A. piles of white salt and other traces of chemicals
    B. Dr. Jekyll, alive but weak
    C. an envelope addressed to Mr. Utterson
    D. Mr. Hyde, dead

10. Which statement is true?
    A. Dr. Jekyll was all good, and Mr. Hyde was all evil.
    B. Dr. Jekyll and Mr. Hyde were both combinations of good and evil.
    C. Dr. Jekyll was all good, but Mr. Hyde was a compound of good and evil.
    D. Dr. Jekyll was still a compound of good and evil, but Mr. Hyde was totally evil.

Multiple Choice Unit Test 2 *The Strange Case of Dr. Jekyll and Mr. Hyde*

III. Quotations

Directions: Write the letter for the speaker on the answer sheet.

A. Dr. Jekyll	B. Mr. Hyde	C. Mr. Utterson	D. Poole
E. Dr. Lanyon	F. Mr. Enfield	G. Mr. Guest	H. Housekeeper

1. "He began to go wrong, wrong in mind; and though of course I continue to take an interest in him for old time's sake, as they say, I see and I have seen devilish little of the man. Such unscientific balderdash would have estranged Damon and Pythias."

2. "Have you got it? Have you got it?"

3. "If he be Mr. Hyde, I shall be Mr. Seek."

4. "I thought it was madness, and now I begin to fear it is disgrace."

5. "If you choose to make a capital out of this accident, I am naturally helpless. No gentleman but wishes to avoid a scene. Name your figure."

6. "Ah! He is in trouble! What has he done?"

7. "Well sir, there's a rather singular resemblance; the two hands are in many points identical: only differently sloped."

8. "I have had a shock," and I shall never recover. It is a question of weeks. Well, life has been pleasant; I liked it; yes, sir, I used to like it. I sometimes think if we knew all, we should be more glad to get away."

9. "I think there's been foul play."

10. "Did you ever remark that door? It is connected in my mind with a very odd story."

Multiple Choice Unit Test 2 *The Strange Case of Dr. Jekyll and Mr. Hyde*

IV. Vocabulary Part 1

1. capacious
2. aversions
3. incongruous
4. inveterately
5. endowed
6. incipient
7. exorbitant
8. disconsolate
9. sedulously
10. ruminated

A. firm dislikes
B. beginning; in an early stage
C. diligently
D. provided
E. absurd; incompatible
F. excessive
G. deep rooted; habitually
H. large
I. pondered; reflected over and over
J. sad

Vocabulary Part 2   Directions: Circle the letter next to the word that matches the definition.

11. **without feeling**
    a. austere
    b. incongruous
    c. volatile
    d. insensate

12. **lean and angular**
    a. endowed
    b. gaunt
    c. multifarious
    d. incipient

13. **power to produce the desired effect**
    a. pecuniary
    b. efficacy
    c. disconsolate
    d. odious

14. **evaporating rapidly**
    a. abject
    b. exorbitant
    c. capacious
    d. volatile

15. **puzzles**
    a. ruminated
    b. lamentation
    c. enigmas
    d. aversions

16. **hateful**
    a. odious
    b. abject
    c. insensate
    d. mien

17. **varied; greatly diversified**
    a. capacious
    b. perplexity
    c. multifarious
    d. eminently

18. **disaster**
    a. perennial
    b. calamity
    c. disinterred
    d. protégé

19. **behavior; bearing**
    a. odious
    b. pecuniary
    c. mien
    d. incipient

20. **domineering; arrogant**
    a. imperious
    b. capacious
    c. multifarious
    d. disconsolate

ANSWER SHEET Multiple Choice Unit Tests
The Strange Case of Dr. Jekyll and Mr. Hyde

I. Matching	III. Quotations	IV. Vocabulary Part 1
1.	1.	1.
2.	2.	2.
3.	3.	3.
4.	4.	4.
5.	5.	5.
6.	6.	6.
7.	7.	7.
8.	8.	8.
9.	9.	9.
10.	10.	10.

II. Multiple Choice

1. (A) (B) (C) (D)
2. (A) (B) (C) (D)
3. (A) (B) (C) (D)
4. (A) (B) (C) (D)
5. (A) (B) (C) (D)
6. (A) (B) (C) (D)
7. (A) (B) (C) (D)
8. (A) (B) (C) (D)
9. (A) (B) (C) (D)
10. (A) (B) (C) (D)

Vocabulary Part 2

11.
12.
13.
14.
15.
16.
17.
18.
19.
20.

ANSWER SHEET KEY Multiple Choice Unit Test 1
The Strange Case of Dr. Jekyll and Mr. Hyde

I. Matching
1. E
2. A
3. G
4. C
5. I
6. F
7. D
8. J
9. B
10. H

II. Multiple Choice
1. ( ) (B) (C) (D)
2. (A) ( ) (C) (D)
3. (A) (B) (C) ( )
4. ( ) (B) (C) (D)
5. (A) (B) ( ) (D)
6. (A) ( ) (C) (D)
7. ( ) (B) (C) (D)
8. (A) (B) (C) ( )
9. (A) (B) ( ) (D)
10. ( ) (B) (C) (D)

III. Quotations
1. F
2. B
3. C
4. C
5. E
6. H
7. G
8. E
9. D
10. A

IV. Vocabulary Part 1
1. J
2. E
3. B
4. G
5. D
6. I
7. A
8. F
9. H
10. C

Vocabulary Part 2
11. C
12. B
13. C
14. D
15. B
16. D
17. D
18. C
19. A
20. C

ANSWER SHEET KEY Multiple Choice Unit Test 2
The Strange Case of Dr. Jekyll and Mr. Hyde

I. Matching		III. Quotations		IV. Vocabulary Part 1	
1.	E	1.	E	1.	H
2.	J	2.	A	2.	A
3.	A	3.	C	3.	E
4.	I	4.	C	4.	G
5.	B	5.	B	5.	D
6.	H	6.	H	6.	B
7.	C	7.	G	7.	F
8.	G	8.	E	8.	J
9.	D	9.	D	9.	C
10.	F	10.	F	10.	I

II. Multiple Choice

1. (A) (B) ( ) (D)
2. (A) ( ) (C) (D)
3. ( ) (B) (C) (D)
4. (A) (B) (C) ( )
5. (A) (B) ( ) (D)
6. (A) (B) (C) ( )
7. (A) (B) ( ) (D)
8. ( ) (B) (C) (D)
9. (A) ( ) (C) (D)
10. (A) (B) (C) ( )

Vocabulary Part 2

11. D
12. B
13. B
14. D
15. C
16. A
17. C
18. B
19. C
20. A

UNIT RESOURCE MATERIALS

BULLETIN BOARD IDEAS - *Dr. Jekyll and Mr. Hyde*

1. Save one corner of the board for the best of students' writing assignments. you may want to use background maps of London to represent the setting of the novel.

2. Draw one of the word search puzzles onto the bulletin board. (Be sure to enlarge it.) Write the key words to one side. Invite students to take their pens or markers and find the words before and/or after class (or perhaps this could be an activity for students who finish their work early).

3. Create a collage of art work from students that conveys their impressions of the characters in this story.

4. Invite students to make an interactive bulletin board quiz. Give each student a half-sheet of paper folded in half so that it can open. On the outside flap, have each student write a description of one of the characters in the text. On the inside, they will write the name of the character. You can staple or tack these papers to the bulletin board so the students can read the descriptions and lift the flaps to find the answers. It works with other things besides characters, too.

5. Make a display of book jackets and articles about *Dr. Jekyll and Mr. Hyde* and Robert Louis Stevenson.

6. Post background paper and let students write their favorite quotes from the book on it.

EXTRA ACTIVITIES *Dr. Jekyll and Mr. Hyde*

One of the difficulties in teaching a novel is that all students don't read at the same speed. One student who likes to read may take the book home and finish it in a day or two. Sometimes a few students finish the in-class assignments early. The problem, then, is finding suitable extra activities for students.

One thing you can do is to keep a little library in the classroom. For this unit on *Dr. Jekyll and Mr. Hyde*, you might check out from the school library other books by Robert Louis Stevenson. A biography of the author would be interesting for some students. Several journals have articles about Stevenson's works. Some students may enjoy reading these and responding either in writing or in discussion groups. Books or articles about related topics, noted earlier in this unit, would be good to have on hand, too.

Other things you may keep on hand are puzzles. We have made some relating directly to *Dr. Jekyll and Mr. Hyde* for you. Feel free to duplicate them for your class.

Some students may like to draw. You might devise a contest or allow some extra-credit grade for students who draw characters or scenes from *Dr. Jekyll and Mr. Hyde*. Note, too, that if the students do not want to keep their drawings you may pick up some extra bulletin board materials this way.

The pages which follow contain games, puzzles and worksheets. The keys, when appropriate, immediately follow the puzzle or worksheet. There are two main groups of activities: one group for the unit; that is, generally relating to the *Dr. Jekyll and Mr. Hyde* text, and another group of activities related strictly to the *Dr. Jekyll and Mr. Hyde* vocabulary.

Directions for the games, puzzles and worksheets are self-explanatory. The object here is to provide you with extra materials you may use in any way you choose.

Dr. Jekyll & Mr. Hyde Word Search

```
P A R L I A M E N T S E U G J O H N X
N X L A N Y O N B O W C B X E L D J S
D I O P L D R H H J O M O G K Z R C '
F E N F I R E O N A L I G T Y W U A T
B D D T G K W N E N L D A G L V G V N
R I O X H Z A F M U A N I P L A S E E
A N N G N N R Q O A G I E G G W N D G
D B P L I K D H C R N G T D R A W D E
S U U E N V F H W Y O H Y V E V B I R
H R R I E P Q Y E B S T E X E N B S O
A G P T T S R M N L R F H N N K Z H N
W H L S Y N R D Y P E L H A F Z V P E
Y Y E A E M W A H W T Q J Z R I O H H
R I C H A R D D R N T E R R O R E R U
W P Z N A N D W Q H U E P K T L Y L N
X A B L U T B N R F Z M N L O C C X D
L H L S X S R E V N A D A O P M A W R
V I B K I B E E C I G N P Q X P N H E
W R E D S T H Y D E D E I G H T E S D
```

BRADSHAW	GALLOWS	MAID	RICHARD
CANE	GREEN	MAW	SCOTLAND
CAVENDISH	GUEST	MIDNIGHT	SIX
DANVERS	HARRY	NEWCOMEN	SOHO
DENMAN	HASTIE	NINETY	SUNDAY
DRAWER	HATRED	NINTH	TEN
DRUGS	HENRY	ONE HUNDRED	TERROR
EDINBURGH	HYDE	PARLIAMENT	THREE
EDWARD	JANUARY	POOLE	UTTERSON
EIGHT	JEKYLL	PORTLAND	WALKS
ENFIELD	JOHN	PURPLE	WILL
FIRE	LANYON	RED	
GAIETY	LONDON	REGENT'S	

Dr. Jekyll & Mr. Hyde Word Search Answer Key

```
P A R L I A M E N T S E U G J O H N
N L A N Y O N   O W C     E   D   S
  I       D R   H J M O   K   R   '
  E   F I R E O N O L I G T Y   C T
B D D T     W   E L D A   L   G V N
R I O   H   A   M U N I   L   S E E
A N N   N   R   O A G E   G   N N G
D B P   I   D   C R N T D R A W D E
S U U E N       W Y O H Y E E   I R
H R R I T       Y   S T   E N   S O
A G P L R   Y   E N R E   N A   H N
W H L S Y N Y   N R E     A R   P E
    E A E   A     E T     R I   H
R I C H A R D   T E R R O R E   U
W         N     H U E   M N L T Y N
  A       L U T   R   M N L O C   D
    L S X S R E V N A D A O M A W R
      I   K I   E E   I   N P   N E
W R E D S     H Y D E D E I G H T E D
```

BRADSHAW	GALLOWS	MAID	RICHARD
CANE	GREEN	MAW	SCOTLAND
CAVENDISH	GUEST	MIDNIGHT	SIX
DANVERS	HARRY	NEWCOMEN	SOHO
DENMAN	HASTIE	NINETY	SUNDAY
DRAWER	HATRED	NINTH	TEN
DRUGS	HENRY	ONE HUNDRED	TERROR
EDINBURGH	HYDE	PARLIAMENT	THREE
EDWARD	JANUARY	POOLE	UTTERSON
EIGHT	JEKYLL	PORTLAND	WALKS
ENFIELD	JOHN	PURPLE	WILL
FIRE	LANYON	RED	
GAIETY	LONDON	REGENT'S	

Dr. Jekyll & Mr. Hyde Crossword Puzzle

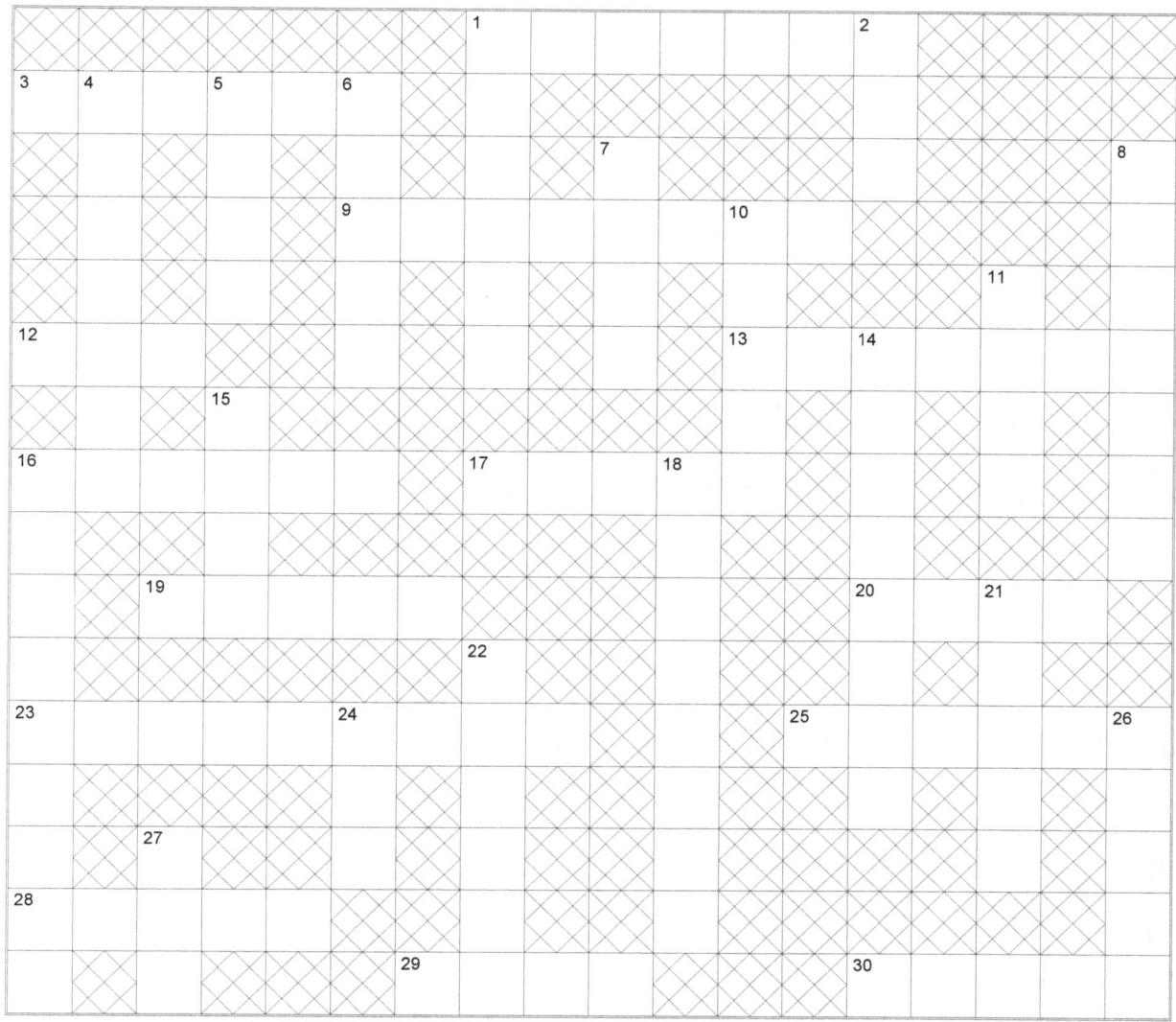

Across
1. First name of murdered man
3. Surgical theater
9. Inspector
12. First color of the liquid
13. Mr. Utterson's first name
16. Mr. Hyde's first name
17. Identified similarity in writings
19. Dr. Jekyll's first name
20. Location of Mr. Hyde's house
23. ____House: Mr. Enfield's name for the residence
25. Dr. Jekyll and Mr. Hyde felt this for each other
28. Third color of the liquid/cheque book color
29. Pure evil
30. Mr. Utterson and Mr. Enfield took them

Down
1. Dr. Lanyon held it for Dr. Jekyll
2. Hours Dr. Jekyll could go before changing to Mr. Hyde
4. Saw Mr. Hyde trample a girl
5. Witnessed the murder
6. Dr. Lanyon received the letter on this date
7. Mr. Utterson's middle name
8. Hyde feared this
10. ____or ten: trampled girl's age
11. Mr. Utterson took the cheque book from the ___
14. Footman
15. Murder weapon
16. Dr. Jekyll's accent
18. The Inspector worked at_____Yard
21. Dr. Jekyll's nickname
22. Pounds fro which the cheque was written
24. Messrs.____:wholesale chemists
26. Caused the change from Jekyll to Hyde
27. Number of years Dr. Lanyon had not seen Dr. Jekyll

Dr. Jekyll & Mr. Hyde Crossword Answer Key

						1 D	A	N	V	E	R	2 S			
3 D	4 E	N	5 M	A	6 N							I			
	N		A		I			7 J			X			8 G
	F		I	9 N	E	W	C	O	10 M	E	N				A
	I		D	T				E		H		I		11 F	L
12 R	E	D		H				R		N		13 G	14 A	B	R	I	E	L
	L		15 C							H			R		R			O
16 E	D	W	A	R	D		17 G	U	E	18 S	T		A		E			W
D			N							C			D					S
I		19 H	E	N	R	Y				O			20 S	O	21 H	O	
N						22 N				T			H		A		
23 B	L	A	C	K	24 M	A	I	L		25 L			H	A	T	R	E	26 D
U					A			N		A			W		R			R
R		27 T			W			E		N			Y				U
28 G	R	E	E	N				T		D							
H		N			29 H	Y	D	E				30 W	A	L	K	S

Across
1. First name of murdered man
3. Surgical theater
9. Inspector
12. First color of the liquid
13. Mr. Utterson's first name
16. Mr. Hyde's first name
17. Identified similarity in writings
19. Dr. Jekyll's first name
20. Location of Mr. Hyde's house
23. ____House: Mr. Enfield's name for the residence
25. Dr. Jekyll and Mr. Hyde felt this for each other
28. Third color of the liquid/cheque book color
29. Pure evil
30. Mr. Utterson and Mr. Enfield took them

Down
1. Dr. Lanyon held it for Dr. Jekyll
2. Hours Dr. Jekyll could go before changing to Mr. Hyde
4. Saw Mr. Hyde trample a girl
5. Witnessed the murder
6. Dr. Lanyon received the letter on this date
7. Mr. Utterson's middle name
8. Hyde feared this
10. ____or ten: trampled girl's age
11. Mr. Utterson took the cheque book from the ___
14. Footman
15. Murder weapon
16. Dr. Jekyll's accent
18. The Inspector worked at _____ Yard
21. Dr. Jekyll's nickname
22. Pounds fro which the cheque was written
24. Messrs.____:wholesale chemists
26. Caused the change from Jekyll to Hyde
27. Number of years Dr. Lanyon had not seen Dr. Jekyll

MATCHING QUIZ/WORKSHEET 1 - DR. JEKYLL AND MR. HYDE

___ 1. GALLOWS	A. Second color of the liquid
___ 2. LONDON	B. ____Park: Dr. Jekyll involuntarily changed to Mr. Hyde here
___ 3. UTTERSON	C. Footman
___ 4. SOHO	D. Hyde feared this
___ 5. JEKYLL	E. Dr. Lanyon received the letter on this date
___ 6. NINTH	F. Murder weapon
___ 7. CAVENDISH	G. Inspector
___ 8. NINETY	H. Identified similarity in writings
___ 9. MAID	I. Dr. Jekyll's servant
___10. JANUARY	J. First name of murdered man
___11. GUEST	K. Dr. Jekyll's lawyer
___12. POOLE	L. Mr. Utterson's middle name
___13. DANVERS	M. Pounds fro which the cheque was written
___14. NEWCOMEN	N. Mr. Utterson dined at Dr. Jekyll's in this month
___15. SCOTLAND	O. # of years Dr. Lanyon had not seen Dr. Jekyll
___16. JOHN	P. The Inspector worked at_____Yard
___17. CANE	Q. Witnessed the murder
___18. TEN	R. Location of Mr. Hyde's house
___19. PURPLE	S. AM time when girl was trampled
___20. REGENT'S	T. First color of the liquid
___21. SIX	U. Combination of good and evil
___22. RED	V. Hours Dr. Jekyll could go before changing to Mr. Hyde
___23. BRADSHAW	W. ____Square: location of De. Lanyon's home
___24. THREE	X. Setting of novel
___25. HOUSEKEEPER	Y. Was glad Mr. Hyde was in trouble

KEY: MATCHING QUIZ/WORKSHEET 1 - DR. JEKYLL AND MR. HYDE

- D - 1. GALLOWS
- X - 2. LONDON
- K - 3. UTTERSON
- R - 4. SOHO
- U - 5. JEKYLL
- E - 6. NINTH
- W - 7. CAVENDISH
- M - 8. NINETY
- Q - 9. MAID
- N - 10. JANUARY
- H - 11. GUEST
- I - 12. POOLE
- J - 13. DANVERS
- G - 14. NEWCOMEN
- P - 15. SCOTLAND
- L - 16. JOHN
- F - 17. CANE
- O - 18. TEN
- A - 19. PURPLE
- B - 20. REGENT'S
- V - 21. SIX
- T - 22. RED
- C - 23. BRADSHAW
- S - 24. THREE
- Y - 25. HOUSEKEEPER

A. Second color of the liquid
B. ____Park: Dr. Jekyll involuntarily changed to Mr. Hyde here
C. Footman
D. Hyde feared this
E. Dr. Lanyon received the letter on this date
F. Murder weapon
G. Inspector
H. Identified similarity in writings
I. Dr. Jekyll's servant
J. First name of murdered man
K. Dr. Jekyll's lawyer
L. Mr. Utterson's middle name
M. Pounds fro which the cheque was written
N. Mr. Utterson dined at Dr. Jekyll's in this month
O. # of years Dr. Lanyon had not seen Dr. Jekyll
P. The Inspector worked at ____ Yard
Q. Witnessed the murder
R. Location of Mr. Hyde's house
S. AM time when girl was trampled
T. First color of the liquid
U. Combination of good and evil
V. Hours Dr. Jekyll could go before changing to Mr. Hyde
W. ____Square: location of De. Lanyon's home
X. Setting of novel
Y. Was glad Mr. Hyde was in trouble

MATCHING QUIZ/WORKSHEET 2 - DR. JEKYLL AND MR. HYDE

___ 1. MIDNIGHT   A. Witnessed the murder
___ 2. WALKS   B. AM time when girl was trampled
___ 3. HYDE   C. Second color of the liquid
___ 4. BRADSHAW   D. Dr. Jekyll's servant
___ 5. NINTH   E. time of murder/time the messenger came
___ 6. THREE   F. Identified similarity in writings
___ 7. HASTIE   G. Disagreed with Dr. Jekyll's methods
___ 8. POOLE   H. Footman
___ 9. ENFIELD   I. Saw Mr. Hyde trample a girl
___10. PURPLE   J. # of years Dr. Lanyon had not seen Dr. Jekyll
___11. EDINBURGH   K. Setting of novel
___12. CHEQUE BOOK   L. Dr. Lanyon received the letter on this date
___13. HATRED   M. Sir Danvers Carew was a member of _____.
___14. TERROR   N. Dr. Jekyll and Mr. Hyde felt this for each other
___15. DANVERS   O. Messrs.____:wholesale chemists
___16. LONDON   P. Dr. Lanyon felt this after his discovery
___17. PARLIAMENT   Q. Dr. Jekyll's accent
___18. MAID   R. Pure evil
___19. DRAWER   S. Mr. Utterson took it from the fire
___20. MAW   T. First name of murdered man
___21. GREEN   U. Mr. Utterson and Mr. Enfield took them
___22. TEN   V. Dr. Lanyon's first name
___23. NEWCOMEN   W. Inspector
___24. GUEST   X. Third color of the liquid/cheque book color
___25. LANYON   Y. Dr. Lanyon held it for Dr. Jekyll

KEY: MATCHING QUIZ/WORKSHEET 2 - DR. JEKYLL AND MR. HYDE

E - 1. MIDNIGHT — A. Witnessed the murder
U - 2. WALKS — B. AM time when girl was trampled
R - 3. HYDE — C. Second color of the liquid
H - 4. BRADSHAW — D. Dr. Jekyll's servant
L - 5. NINTH — E. time of murder/time the messenger came
B - 6. THREE — F. Identified similarity in writings
V - 7. HASTIE — G. Disagreed with Dr. Jekyll's methods
D - 8. POOLE — H. Footman
I - 9. ENFIELD — I. Saw Mr. Hyde trample a girl
C - 10. PURPLE — J. # of years Dr. Lanyon had not seen Dr. Jekyll
Q - 11. EDINBURGH — K. Setting of novel
S - 12. CHEQUE BOOK — L. Dr. Lanyon received the letter on this date
N - 13. HATRED — M. Sir Danvers Carew was a member of _____.
P - 14. TERROR — N. Dr. Jekyll and Mr. Hyde felt this for each other
T - 15. DANVERS — O. Messrs. ____ :wholesale chemists
K - 16. LONDON — P. Dr. Lanyon felt this after his discovery
M - 17. PARLIAMENT — Q. Dr. Jekyll's accent
A - 18. MAID — R. Pure evil
Y - 19. DRAWER — S. Mr. Utterson took it from the fire
O - 20. MAW — T. First name of murdered man
X - 21. GREEN — U. Mr. Utterson and Mr. Enfield took them
J - 22. TEN — V. Dr. Lanyon's first name
W - 23. NEWCOMEN — W. Inspector
F - 24. GUEST — X. Third color of the liquid/cheque book color
G - 25. LANYON — Y. Dr. Lanyon held it for Dr. Jekyll

JUGGLE LETTER REVIEW GAME CLUE SHEET - DR. JEKYLL AND MR. HYDE

1. USDGR = 1. _____
   Caused the change from Jekyll to Hyde

2. RENEG = 2. _____
   Third color of the liquid/cheque book color

3. MENAND = 3. _____
   Surgical theater

4. AIEGYT = 4. _____
   Dr. Jekyll didn't like it about himself

5. EQUKHE CBOO = 5. _____
   Mr. Utterson took it from the fire

6. RDNSAVE = 6. _____
   First name of murdered man

7. RHRAY = 7. _____
   Dr. Jekyll's nickname

8. LILW = 8. _____
   Mr. Utterson had Dr. Jekyll's

9. DOCATLSN = 9. _____
   The Inspector worked at_____Yard

10. DNLOON =10. _____
    Setting of novel

11. YNNEIT =11. _____
    Pounds fro which the cheque was written

12. OAGWLLS =12. _____
    Hyde feared this

13. SEUTG =13. _____
    Identified similarity in writings

14. NCEA =14. _____
    Murder weapon

15. WDEARR =15. _____
    Dr. Lanyon held it for Dr. Jekyll

16. YLKJLE =16. _____
Combination of good and evil

17. DAYUSN =17. _____
Mr. Utterson and Mr. Enfield's walking day

18. AMW =18. _____
Messrs.____:wholesale chemists

19. OSEEHREUKPE =19. _____
Was glad Mr. Hyde was in trouble

20. NNOEERHU DD =20. _____
Pounds Mr. Hyde gave the family

21. OSOH =21. _____
Location of Mr. Hyde's house

22. HADCVNIES =22. _____
____Square: location of De. Lanyon's home

23. HTEER =23. _____
AM time when girl was trampled

24. REOTRR =24. _____
Dr. Lanyon felt this after his discovery

25. AIGERLB =25. _____
Mr. Utterson's first name

26. LWAKS =26. _____
Mr. Utterson and Mr. Enfield took them

27. IELNDFE =27. _____
Saw Mr. Hyde trample a girl

28. AMDI =28. _____
Witnessed the murder

29. CKLMLBAIA =29. _____
____House: Mr. Enfield's name for the residence

30. HJON =30. _____
Mr. Utterson's middle name

31. ASHIET =31. _____
   Dr. Lanyon's first name

32. SBDARHAW =32. _____
   Footman

33. EOPOL =33. _____
   Dr. Jekyll's servant

34. AOLNYN =34. _____
   Disagreed with Dr. Jekyll's methods

35. HITGMNID =35. _____
   time of murder/time the messenger came

36. ERD =36. _____
   First color of the liquid

37. PDARONTL =37. _____
   ____ Street: Mr. Hyde drove to a hotel there

38. PRULEP =38. _____
   Second color of the liquid

39. AETDHR =39. _____
   Dr. Jekyll and Mr. Hyde felt this for each other

40. TEENR'GS =40. _____
   ____Park: Dr. Jekyll involuntarily changed to Mr. Hyde here

41. WRDDEA =41. _____
   Mr. Hyde's first name

42. RNAAJYU =42. _____
   Mr. Utterson dined at Dr. Jekyll's in this month

43. NTE =43. _____
   # of years Dr. Lanyon had not seen Dr. Jekyll

44. RHYEN =44. _____
   Dr. Jekyll's first name

45. EYHD =45. _____
   Pure evil

KEY: JUGGLE LETTER REVIEW GAME CLUE SHEET - DR. JEKYLL AND MR. HYDE

1. USDGR = 1. DRUGS
Caused the change from Jekyll to Hyde

2. RENEG = 2. GREEN
Third color of the liquid/cheque book color

3. MENAND = 3. DENMAN
Surgical theater

4. AIEGYT = 4. GAIETY
Dr. Jekyll didn't like it about himself

5. EQUKHE CBOO = 5. CHEQUE BOOK
Mr. Utterson took it from the fire

6. RDNSAVE = 6. DANVERS
First name of murdered man

7. RHRAY = 7. HARRY
Dr. Jekyll's nickname

8. LILW = 8. WILL
Mr. Utterson had Dr. Jekyll's

9. DOCATLSN = 9. SCOTLAND
The Inspector worked at_____Yard

10. DNLOON =10. LONDON
Setting of novel

11. YNNEIT =11. NINETY
Pounds fro which the cheque was written

12. OAGWLLS =12. GALLOWS
Hyde feared this

13. SEUTG =13. GUEST
Identified similarity in writings

14. NCEA =14. CANE
Murder weapon

15. WDEARR =15. DRAWER
Dr. Lanyon held it for Dr. Jekyll

16. YLKJLE =16. JEKYLL
Combination of good and evil

17. DAYUSN =17. SUNDAY
Mr. Utterson and Mr. Enfield's walking day

18. AMW =18. MAW
Messrs.____:wholesale chemists

19. OSEEHREUKPE =19. HOUSEKEEPER
Was glad Mr. Hyde was in trouble

20. NNOEERHU DD =20. ONE HUNDRED
Pounds Mr. Hyde gave the family

21. OSOH =21. SOHO
Location of Mr. Hyde's house

22. HADCVNIES =22. CAVENDISH
____Square: location of De. Lanyon's home

23. HTEER =23. THREE
AM time when girl was trampled

24. REOTRR =24. TERROR
Dr. Lanyon felt this after his discovery

25. AIGERLB =25. GABRIEL
Mr. Utterson's first name

26. LWAKS =26. WALKS
Mr. Utterson and Mr. Enfield took them

27. IELNDFE =27. ENFIELD
Saw Mr. Hyde trample a girl

28. AMDI =28. MAID
Witnessed the murder

29. CKLMLBAIA =29. BLACK MAIL
____House: Mr. Enfield's name for the residence

30. HJON =30. JOHN
Mr. Utterson's middle name

31. ASHIET =31. HASTIE
Dr. Lanyon's first name

32. SBDARHAW =32. BRADSHAW
Footman

33. EOPOL =33. POOLE
Dr. Jekyll's servant

34. AOLNYN =34. LANYON
Disagreed with Dr. Jekyll's methods

35. HITGMNID =35. MIDNIGHT
time of murder/time the messenger came

36. ERD =36. RED
First color of the liquid

37. PDARONTL =37. PORTLAND
____ Street: Mr. Hyde drove to a hotel there

38. PRULEP =38. PURPLE
Second color of the liquid

39. AETDHR =39. HATRED
Dr. Jekyll and Mr. Hyde felt this for each other

40. TEENR'GS =40. REGENT'S
____Park: Dr. Jekyll involuntarily changed to Mr. Hyde here

41. WRDDEA =41. EDWARD
Mr. Hyde's first name

42. RNAAJYU =42. JANUARY
Mr. Utterson dined at Dr. Jekyll's in this month

43. NTE =43. TEN
# of years Dr. Lanyon had not seen Dr. Jekyll

44. RHYEN =44. HENRY
Dr. Jekyll's first name

45. EYHD =45. HYDE
Pure evil

VOCABULARY RESOURCE MATERIALS

Dr. Jekyll & Mr. Hyde Vocabulary Word Search

```
I N V E T E R A T E L Y W S I B E F U
M I L F A C C O S T E D T O N I N V U
P N V Y R Z A T E C K C H M C N I D O
E C G C H M J P T F R X V B I I G E B
R O M N R H G D A N V U T R P Q M T T
I N X E L X F T S C Y E T E I U A E R
O G X R S P D Z N P I X X I E I S S U
U R Y E Y Y F I E V E O P Y N T D T S
S U R H R E P O S E X R U Q T Y Z A I
N O A O X O N N N I O B P S H R B B V
X U I C T D O Z I T N I M L C J P L E
W S N N J I Z E E C W T C I E Q S E M
K W U I S O A G F D O A E C E X T L D
V A C R M U E U E F L N T R J N I I Y
G Q E P H S J W S A I T D P R Q K T N
J V P D Q R O X M T Z C Y O H E M A Y
A P P Z Y D K I Q T E X A Y N C D L Q
R U M I N A T E D D H R F C F E X O N
V F B E V Y R E P R O V E Z Y P D V P
```

ABJECT	EFFICACY	INIQUITY	REPROVE
ACCOSTED	ENDOWED	INSENSATE	RUMINATED
AUSTERE	ENIGMAS	INVETERATELY	SCRUTINY
AVERSIONS	EXORBITANT	MIEN	SOMBRE
CALAMITY	GAUNT	ODIOUS	UNOBTRUSIVE
CAPACIOUS	IMPERIOUS	PECUNIARY	VOLATILE
CONDONED	INCIPIENT	PERPLEXITY	
DETESTABLE	INCOHERENCY	PROTEGE	
DISINTERRED	INCONGRUOUS	REPOSE	

Dr. Jekyll & Mr. Hyde Vocabulary Word Search Answer Key

```
I N V E T E R A T E L Y     S     E     U
M I     A C C O S T E D     O  I  N     N
P N  Y     A     E   C      M  C  I  D  O
E C  C     P     C   R      B  I  G  E  B
R O  N     T     R   U      R  P  M  T  T
I N  E     A     E   E  T   E  I  A  E  R
O G  R     D  N  P  I X     I  E  S  S  U
U R  E        I  E   O P    E  N  T  T  S
S U  H  R  E  P  O S E R  U T   Y     A  I
 O   O     O  N  I   B P S        B   B  V
 U   C     D  O  I   T N I M      J   L  E
 S   T     I  E   C  T C I E         E
     N  S  O  A  G F D O A  C E X    L
     U  I     U  E F L N T  R   N    I
  G  E  R     S  W A I T D  R        T
     V  P        O  M T  C  O   E    A Y
  A        D        I    E  A   D    L
  R U M I N A T E D      R  C   E    O
           E  Y R E P R O V E   Y    D V
```

ABJECT   EFFICACY   INIQUITY   REPROVE

ACCOSTED   ENDOWED   INSENSATE   RUMINATED

AUSTERE   ENIGMAS   INVETERATELY   SCRUTINY

AVERSIONS   EXORBITANT   MIEN   SOMBRE

CALAMITY   GAUNT   ODIOUS   UNOBTRUSIVE

CAPACIOUS   IMPERIOUS   PECUNIARY   VOLATILE

CONDONED   INCIPIENT   PERPLEXITY

DETESTABLE   INCOHERENCY   PROTEGE

DISINTERRED   INCONGRUOUS   REPOSE

Dr. Jekyll & Mr. Hyde Vocabulary Crossword

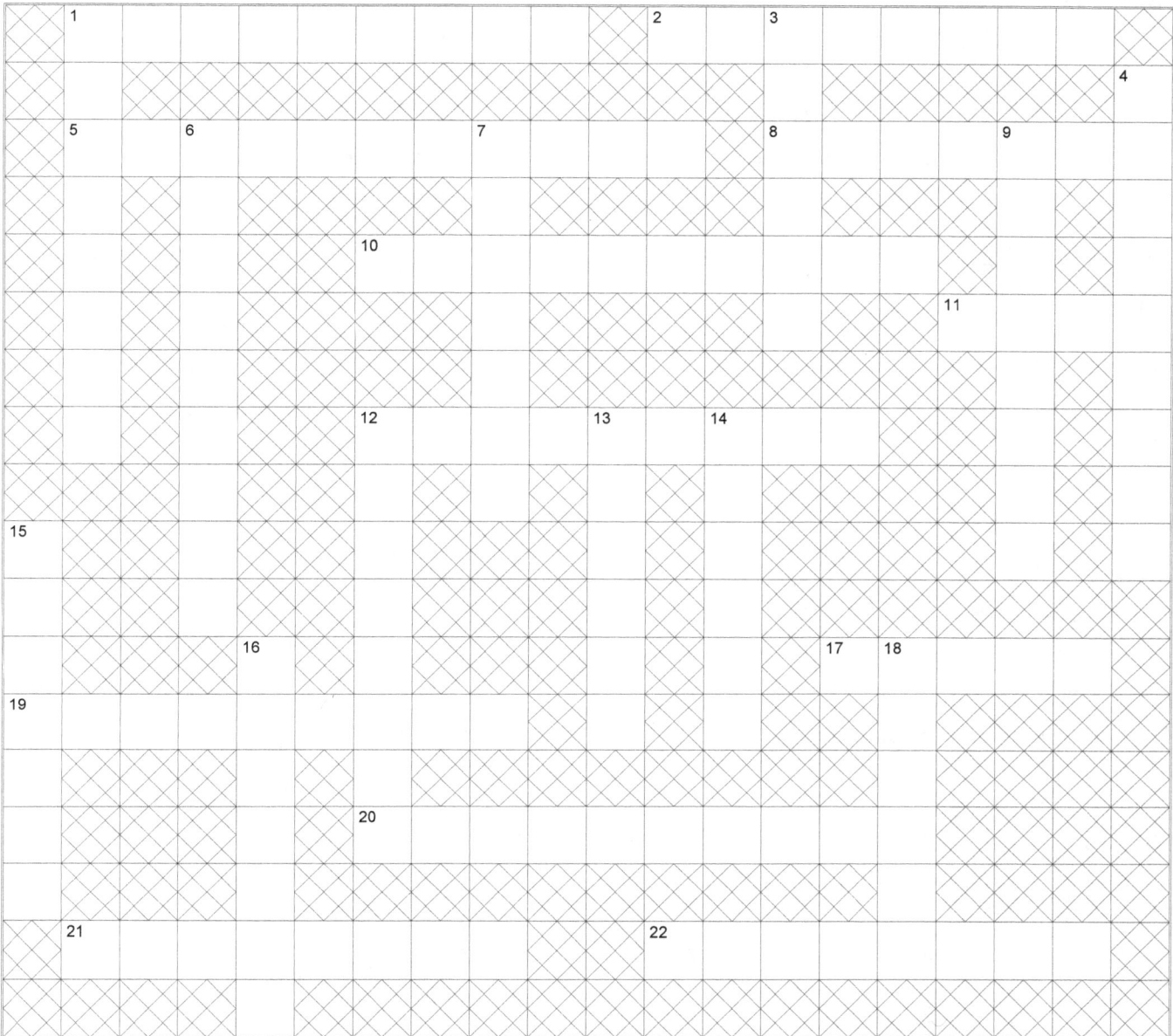

Across
1. Beginning; in an early stage
2. Close examination
5. Unable to express one's thoughts clearly
8. A person under the support of a patron
10. Diligently
11. Behavior; bearing
12. Firm dislike
17. Lean and angler
19. Pondered; reflected over and over
20. Hateful; nasty
21. Disaster
22. Evaporating rapidly

Down
1. Wickedness; injustice
3. To place trust in
4. Relating to money
6. Large
7. Provided
9. Power to produce the desired effect
12. Spoke to first
13. Gloomy; depressing
14. Hateful
15. Rebuke; scold
16. Puzzles
18. Wretched; lacking pride

Dr. Jekyll & Mr. Hyde Vocabulary Crossword Answer Key

```
1:  I N C I P I E N T   2:S C R U T I N Y
    N                     E             4:P
5:I N6:C O H E R7:E N C Y 8:P R O T9:E G E
    Q   A         N         O       F   C
    U   P   10:S E D U L O U S L Y F   U
    I   A         O         E   11:M I E N
    T   C         W                 C   I
    Y   I   12:A V13:E R14:S I O N S A   A
        O       C   D   O   D       C   R
15:R    U       C   O   M   I       Y   Y
E       S       O   B   O
P           16:E S   R   U   17:G18:A U N T
19:R U M I N A T E D E   S   B
O           I       E       J
V           G   20:D E T E S T A B L E
E           M                       C
    21:C A L A M I T Y   22:V O L A T I L E
            S
```

Across
1. Beginning; in an early stage
2. Close examination
5. Unable to express one's thoughts clearly
8. A person under the support of a patron
10. Diligently
11. Behavior; bearing
12. Firm dislike
17. Lean and angler
19. Pondered; reflected over and over
20. Hateful; nasty
21. Disaster
22. Evaporating rapidly

Down
1. Wickedness; injustice
3. To place trust in
4. Relating to money
6. Large
7. Provided
9. Power to produce the desired effect
12. Spoke to first
13. Gloomy; depressing
14. Hateful
15. Rebuke; scold
16. Puzzles
18. Wretched; lacking pride

VOCABULARY MATCHING *Dr. Jekyll and Mr. Hyde*

_____ 1. eminently
_____ 2. reprove
_____ 3. detestable
_____ 4. perplexity
_____ 5. condoned
_____ 6. unobtrusive
_____ 7. accosted
_____ 8. conflagration
_____ 9. disinterred
_____ 10. ruminated
_____ 11. mien
_____ 12. abject
_____ 13. lamentation
_____ 14. volatile
_____ 15. scrutiny
_____ 16. endowed
_____ 17. inveterately
_____ 18. multifarious
_____ 19. efficacy
_____ 20. pecuniary

A. varied; greatly diversified
B. not noticeable
C. rebuke; scold
D. close examination
E. behavior; bearing
F. relating to money
G. outstanding
H. deep rooted; habitually
I. overlooked; forgiven
J. grieving; expressing sorrow
K. spoke to first
L. confusion; puzzlement
M. evaporating rapidly
N. dug up
O. power to produce the desired effect
P. hateful; nasty
Q. supplied with a quality
R. a great fire
S. wretched; lacking pride
T. pondered; reflected over and over

ANSWER KEY VOCABULARY MATCHING *Dr. Jekyll and Mr. Hyde*

G	1.	eminently	A.	varied; greatly diversified
C	2.	reprove	B.	not noticeable
P	3.	detestable	C.	rebuke; scold
L	4.	perplexity	D.	close examination
I	5.	condoned	E.	behavior; bearing
B	6.	unobtrusive	F.	relating to money
K	7.	accosted	G.	outstanding
R	8.	conflagration	H.	deep rooted; habitually
N	9.	disinterred	I.	overlooked; forgiven
T	10.	ruminated	J.	grieving; expressing sorrow
E	11.	mien	K.	spoke to first
S	12.	abject	L.	confusion; puzzlement
J	13.	lamentation	M.	evaporating rapidly
M	14.	volatile	N.	dug up
D	15.	scrutiny	O.	power to produce the desired effect
Q	16.	endowed	P.	hateful; nasty
H	17.	inveterately	Q.	supplied with a quality
A	18.	multifarious	R.	a great fire
O	19.	efficacy	S.	wretched; lacking pride
F	20.	pecuniary	T.	pondered; reflected over and over

VOCABULARY MULTIPLE CHOICE *Dr. Jekyll and Mr. Hyde*

1. **strict; stern**
   a. reprove
   b. capacious
   c. austere
   d. odious

2. **a person under the support of a patron**
   a. calamity
   b. protégé
   c. gaunt
   d. insensate

3. **wickedness; injustice**
   a. iniquity
   b. conflagration
   c. ruminated
   d. pecuniary

4. **without feeling**
   a. austere
   b. incongruous
   c. volatile
   d. insensate

5. **lean and angular**
   a. endowed
   b. gaunt
   c. multifarious
   d. incipient

6. **sad**
   a. pecuniary
   b. enigmas
   c. disconsolate
   d. reprove

7. **excessive**
   a. abject
   b. *exorbitant*
   c. capacious
   d. volatile

8. **puzzles**
   a. ruminated
   b. lamentation
   c. *enigmas*
   d. aversions

9. **gloomy; depressing**
   a. pecuniary
   b. exorbitant
   c. abject
   d. sombre

10. **to place trust in**
    a. reprove
    b. accosted
    c. scrutiny
    d. repose

11. **unable to express thoughts clearly**
    a. austere
    b. insensate
    c. incoherency
    d. sombre

12. **hateful**
    a. odious
    b. abject
    c. insensate
    d. mien

13. **diligently**
    a. capacious
    b. perplexity
    c. sedulously
    d. eminently

14. **disaster**
    a. perennial
    b. *calamity*
    c. disinterred
    d. protégé

15. **beginning; in an early stage**
    a. odious
    b. pecuniary
    c. mien
    d. *incipient*

16. **domineering; arrogant**
    a. *imperious*
    b. capacious
    c. multifarious
    d. disconsolate

ANSWER KEY VOCABULARY MULTIPLE CHOICE *Dr. Jekyll and Mr. Hyde*

1. **strict; stern**
    a. reprove
    b. capacious
    c. *austere*
    d. odious

2. **a person under the support of a patron**
    a. calamity
    b. *protégé*
    c. gaunt
    d. insensate

3. **wickedness; injustice**
    a. *iniquity*
    b. conflagration
    c. ruminated
    d. pecuniary

4. **without feeling**
    a. austere
    b. incongruous
    c. volatile
    d. *insensate*

5. **lean and angular**
    a. endowed
    b. *gaunt*
    c. multifarious
    d. incipient

6. **sad**
    a. pecuniary
    b. enigmas
    c. *disconsolate*
    d. reprove

7. **excessive**
    a. abject
    b. *exorbitant*
    c. capacious
    d. volatile

8. **puzzles**
    a. ruminated
    b. lamentation
    c. *enigmas*
    d. aversions

9. **gloomy; depressing**
    a. pecuniary
    b. exorbitant
    c. abject
    d. *sombre*

10. **to place trust in**
    a. reprove
    b. accosted
    c. scrutiny
    d. *repose*

11. **unable to express thoughts clearly**
    a. austere
    b. insensate
    c. *incoherency*
    d. sombre

12. **hateful**
    a. *odious*
    b. abject
    c. insensate
    d. mien

13. **diligently**
    a. capacious
    b. perplexity
    c. *sedulously*
    d. eminently

14. **disaster**
    a. perennial
    b. *calamity*
    c. disinterred
    d. protégé

15. **beginning; in an early stage**
    a. odious
    b. pecuniary
    c. mien
    d. *incipient*

16. **domineering; arrogant**
    a. *imperious*
    b. capacious
    c. multifarious
    d. disconsolate

VOCABULARY JUGGLE LETTER REVIEW GAME CLUE SHEET - *Dr. Jekyll*

1. IMORUPSIE = 1. _____
   Domineering; arrogant

2. VRSSNIOAE = 2. _____
   Firm dislike

3. BMOESR = 3. _____
   Gloomy; depressing

4. SETEURA = 4. _____
   Strict; stern

5. YTLMENNIE = 5. _____
   Outstanding

6. UGNTA = 6. _____
   Lean and angler

7. XEBNTTIAOR = 7. _____
   Excessive

8. REEDSNDTIRI = 8. _____
   Dug up

9. LINFORCAAGNOT = 9. _____
   A great fire

10. LASEOIDOTSCN =10. _____
    Sad

11. DTECCOAS =11. _____
    Spoke to first

12. APSOCIUAC =12. _____
    Large

13. YSSLOLEDUU =13. _____
    Diligently

14. ETSNEAINS =14. _____
    Without feeling

15. EPEORRV =15. _____
    Rebuke; scold

16. DOIUSO =16. _____
Hateful

17. AFCYCIFE =17. _____
Power to produce the desired effect

18. EDWEDNO =18. _____
Provided

19. TERSUNIBUOV =19. _____
Not noticeable

20. TYAAIMLC =20. _____
Disaster

21. LEESETDATB =21. _____
Hateful; nasty

22. DEONNDOC =22. _____
Overlooked; forgiven

23. TRNDIUAEM =23. _____
Pondered; reflected over and over

24. GSIOUNONCUR =24. _____
Absurd; incompatible

25. GETRPOE =25. _____
A person under the support of a patron

26. PYTRLIPEEX =26. _____
Confusion; puzzlement

27. LMITORASFUIU =27. _____
Varied; greatly diversified

28. EENLAINRP =28. _____
Continuing; recurring

29. EMNI =29. _____
Behavior; bearing

30. TTNIOENMALA =30. _____
Grieving; expressing sorrow

31. PSEORE =31. _____
To place trust in

32. OALLIETV =32. _____
Evaporating rapidly

33. ITNICNIPE =33. _____
Beginning; in an early stage

34. YNIIITUQ =34. _____
Wickedness; injustice

35. MESIGNA =35. _____
Puzzles

46. NSUTRYCI =46. _____
Close examination

KEY: VOCABULARY JUGGLE LETTER REVIEW GAME CLUE SHEET - *Dr. Jekyll*

1. IMORUPSIE = 1. IMPERIOUS
   Domineering; arrogant

2. VRSSNIOAE = 2. AVERSIONS
   Firm dislike

3. BMOESR = 3. SOMBRE
   Gloomy; depressing

4. SETEURA = 4. AUSTERE
   Strict; stern

5. YTLMENNIE = 5. EMINENTLY
   Outstanding

6. UGNTA = 6. GAUNT
   Lean and angler

7. XEBNTTIAOR = 7. EXORBITANT
   Excessive

8. REEDSNDTIRI = 8. DISINTERRED
   Dug up

9. LINFORCAAGNOT = 9. CONFLAGRATION
   A great fire

10. LASEOIDOTSCN =10. DISCONSOLATE
    Sad

11. DTECCOAS =11. ACCOSTED
    Spoke to first

12. APSOCIUAC =12. CAPACIOUS
    Large

13. YSSLOLEDUU =13. SEDULOUSLY
    Diligently

14. ETSNEAINS =14. INSENSATE
    Without feeling

15. EPEORRV =15. REPROVE
    Rebuke; scold

16. DOIUSO =16. ODIOUS
Hateful

17. AFCYCIFE =17. EFFICACY
Power to produce the desired effect

18. EDWEDNO =18. ENDOWED
Provided

19. TERSUNIBUOV =19. UNOBTRUSIVE
Not noticeable

20. TYAAIMLC =20. CALAMITY
Disaster

21. LEESETDATB =21. DETESTABLE
Hateful; nasty

22. DEONNDOC =22. CONDONED
Overlooked; forgiven

23. TRNDIUAEM =23. RUMINATED
Pondered; reflected over and over

24. GSIOUNONCUR =24. INCONGRUOUS
Absurd; incompatible

25. GETRPOE =25. PROTEGE
A person under the support of a patron

26. PYTRLIPEEX =26. PERPLEXITY
Confusion; puzzlement

27. LMITORASFUIU =27. MULTIFARIOUS
Varied: greatly diversified

28. EENLAINRP =28. PERENNIAL
Continuing: recurring

29. EMNI =29. MIEN
Behavior; bearing

30. TTNIOENMALA =30. LAMENTATION
Grieving; expressing sorrow

31. PSEORE =31. REPOSE
To place trust in

32. OALLIETV =32. VOLATILE
Evaporating rapidly

33. ITNICNIPE =33. INCIPIENT
Beginning; in an early stage

34. YNIIITUQ =34. INIQUITY
Wickedness; injustice

35. MESIGNA =35. ENIGMAS
Puzzles

36. NSUTRYCI =36. SCRUTINY
Close examination

www.ingramcontent.com/pod-product-compliance
Lightning Source LLC
Chambersburg PA
CBHW051412070526
44584CB00023B/3403